GALATIANS

In Defense of the Gospel

By Jack Sequeira

VINEYARD MINISTRIES

Galatians: In Defense of the Gospel
Jack Sequeira

Edited by Edwin A. Schwisow
Cover and Layout by Ron Burgard, Macmouser Graphics

Published by Vineyard Ministries
PMB #244, 3760 Market Street NE
Salem, OR 97301
www.jacksequeira.org

Unless otherwise indicated, Scripture is taken from the *New King James Version.*

Printed in the United States of America

ISBN: 0-9769168-2-7

CC030209

Table of Contents

Dedication

This book
is lovingly dedicated
to Harold & Nelma Drake
in appreciation for their
Christian example,
dedicated leadership, and support of
Marriage Enrichment, Family Life and
Vineyard Ministries

Preface

Approximately 30 years marked the time between the apostle Paul's conversion on the Damascus road to his martyrdom in Rome. During this period he made three major missionary journeys throughout Asia Minor, establishing churches wherever he went, including the province of Galatia.

But wherever Paul established churches, Jewish believers (known as Judaizers) who questioned Paul's apostolic authority would infiltrate these churches and attack his gospel of salvation by grace alone, through faith alone, insisting that Gentile believers add good works and law keeping (including circumcision) as requirements for salvation (Acts 15:1-11).

The church of Galatia fell for this false, or perverted, gospel (Galatians 1:6, 7), and the Epistle to the Galatians is Paul's response. It is the most severe letter he ever penned, with no commendations, no praise, and no thanksgiving. Some scholars describe this epistle as Paul's angry letter.

The Galatian believers who accepted the false teachings of the Judaizers were in grave danger of losing their salvation altogether, since they were in the process of turning their backs on the very foundation of their faith—Jesus Christ and Him crucified (Galatians 5:4). Hence, we can define Paul's Epistle to the Galatians as a "fighting letter."

Paul says that perverting the purity of the gospel is bringing the curse of God on oneself. This is how he expressed it to the Galatian believers: "But even if we (*apostles*) or an angel from heaven should preach a gospel other than the one we preached to you, let him be eternally condemned! As we have already said, so now I say again: If anyone is preaching to you a gospel other than what you accepted, let him be eternally condemned!" (Galatians 1:8, 9).

Many Christians today still face the problems of the Galatian churches, falling into the same trap. While the demands made on them may not be identical to those the Judaizers imposed on the Gentile believers of their day, the outcome is the same, a subtle form of legalism that confuses the incredibly good news of the gospel (what Christ accomplished for mankind in His birth, life, death and resurrection) with Christian living, or sanctification, the application or the fruits of the gospel.

The issues of Epistle to the Galatians are alive and well, for in every age, Satan, the enemy of souls and the gospel, tries to destroy the purity of the gospel, thus robbing God's people of the joy and assurance of salvation in Christ.

Christians living in the 21st century, therefore, desperately need to consider Paul's message to the Galatians. This epistle may be considered as the New Testament's emancipation proclamation from any and every form of legalism. As Paul wrote to the believers in Corinth: "But I am afraid that just as Eve was deceived by the serpent's (*Satan's*) cunning, your minds may somehow be led astray from your sincere and pure devotion to Christ. For if someone comes to you and preaches a Jesus other than the Jesus we (*apostles*) preached, or if you received a different spirit from the one you received, or a different gospel from the one you accepted, you put up with it easily enough (2 Corinthians 11:3, 4). Paul repeats a similar warning in 2 Corinthians 4:3 and 4.

Because Paul's ultimate goal in writing to the believers in Galatia and to all believers who will read his letter throughout the centuries is to protect the purity of the gospel from corrupting influences, I have chosen to subtitle these studies, "In Defense of the Gospel."

The purpose of these expository studies is to protect our modern readers from falling into the same trap as the Galatian Christians did in New Testament times.

To gain the most from each chapter of this book, it is advisable to first read the passage listed below each chapter heading. I am not claiming infallibility, however, and the best I can hope for is that you will be stimulated to seriously and prayerfully consider the warnings and counsel given by Paul to the Christians in Galatia.

Jack Sequeira
www.jacksequeira.org

Chapter 1
The Galatian Problem
Galatians 1:1-10

The Epistle to the Galatians is one of Paul's most important New Testament letters—written early in his Christian ministry in response to a very real emergency.

God had sent His Son to this world, not to condemn it, but to save humanity from the results of Adam's and Eve's rebellion. This truth lies at the core of everything Paul preaches (John 3:16-18).

After Jesus finished His earthly mission and obtained salvation full and complete for all mankind, He commissioned His apostles to go to the entire world and preach the gospel's incredible good news to all mankind—to every creature. All who believed and were baptized would be saved (Mark 16:15 and 16).

Enemy of Souls

But Paul knows there is one who hates the gospel—an enemy of souls who attacks and distorts the gospel message. The apostle writes in 2 Corinthians 4:3 and 4, for example, that if the gospel be hid, it is hid because the god of this world—that is, Satan—has blinded the eyes of those who do not believe, lest they come to the light of the glorious gospel of the Lord, Jesus Christ.

Satan, however, does not confine his efforts to non-Christians. The moment believers accept the gospel and begin rejoicing in Christ, Satan does his utmost to sidetrack them from the pure gospel proclaimed by the apostles. Wherever Paul proclaims the gospel of the Lord, Jesus Christ and establishes churches, a group known as the Judaizers dog his footsteps to undo his good work and rob the new Christians of their freedom in Christ. The Galatian Christians find themselves wavering under just such an attack.

Paul's epistle to them is stern and solemn, with no commendation, no praise, and no thanksgiving. As he writes, the Galatian believers are in the process of accepting the Judaizers' false teachings. They are in grave danger of losing the very foundation of their faith. Paul's Epistle to the Galatians can truly be called a "fighting letter."

Faith and Fruit

Many Christians in all denominations today are falling into a subtle Galatian-like legalism that confuses *faith* with *fruits.* The fruits of justification by faith experienced through the process of sanctification make no contribution whatever to one's entitlement to heaven. These fruits are the evidence of justification by faith (James 2:20-22). Christians today desperately need to consider Paul's message to the Galatians, for this epistle is the New Testament declaration of emancipation from any and every type of legalism (salvation by works). It is the strongest document in all Scripture in defense of justification by faith alone—a doctrine upon which Luther is said to have declared that the church stands or falls.

Paul deals in Galatians with issues that are very much alive today. In every age (ours included) Satan, the enemy of souls, tries to rob God's people of the joy and assurance of salvation by adding works of the law. A true understanding of Galatians offers a powerful safeguard for the purity of the gospel in our age.

Historical Perspective

Some 30 years pass between Paul's conversion on the road to Damascus and his martyrdom in Rome—years that include travel throughout Asia Minor as an ambassador of Jesus Christ.

During his three famous missionary journeys, he preaches the gospel and plants churches in the province of Galatia, in Asia, and in the northern and southern parts of Greece. He follows up these visits with letters of guidance and encouragement—of which the letter to the Galatians, written between 48 and 57 A.D, is one of the earliest.

The Galatian Christians' case is unusual, in that false teachers almost immediately infiltrate the new believers and convince them that Paul is a self-appointed apostle who teaches a gospel at odds with the preaching of the other apostles. As soon as Paul hears about what is going on in Galatia, he writes the new believers this epistle of admonition.

Two Main Themes

We focus in this chapter on the first 10 verses of Galatians. Here Paul touches on the two main themes of this epistle—namely his apostolic authority (which has come under fire) and the content of the gospel that he proclaims.

Paul with great success has established churches in Galatia, but revisionist teachers known as Judaizers are now mounting powerful attacks against his apostolic authority and presentation of the gospel.

These Judaizers are Jewish Christians who believe in Christ as the Messiah but reject Paul's message of salvation by grace alone. They insist that justification is not by faith alone in Jesus Christ. "Oh, yes," we can hear them saying. "The gospel requires faith, but it also requires circumcision, keeping the law, and good works if you are to be saved."

The controversy itself is not new to early Christianity. Some time before, just such a controversy led directly to the convening of the Jerusalem Council recorded in Acts 15.

There we discover that these same Judaizers were insisting that the Gentile Christians had to be circumcised (verse 1) and keep the law (verse 5) to be saved. Both Paul and Barnabas opposed this teaching with all their power and authority. This led the church in Antioch to send delegates (including Paul and Barnabas) to Jerusalem for clarification.

Introduction and Problem

Paul introduces himself and greets his readers in Galatians 1:1-5: "Paul, an apostle, (not from men nor through man, but by Jesus Christ and God the Father who raised him from the dead) and all the brethren who are with me, to the churches of Galatia: Grace to you and peace from God the Father and our Lord Jesus Christ, who gave Himself for our sins, that He might deliver us from this present evil age, according to the will of our God and Father, to whom be glory forever and ever. Amen."

In verses 6-10, then, Paul begins to address the Galatian problem: "I marvel that you are turning away so soon from Him who called you in the grace of Christ, to a different gospel, which is not another; but there are some who trouble you and want to pervert the gospel of Christ. But even if we, or an angel from heaven, preach any other gospel to you than what we have preached to you let him be accursed. As we have said before, so now I say again, if anyone preaches any other gospel to you than what you have received, let him be accursed. For do I now persuade men or God? Or do I seek to please men? For if I still pleased men, I would not be a servant of Christ."

Paul's Apostleship

In the first five verses, Paul introduces himself as an apostle appointed (in parenthesis) "not from men." By "men" in the plural Paul is referring to an apostolic committee—a group such as the one that selected Matthias as an apostle to replace the tragic departure of Judas. Nor is Paul chosen by any "man" (singular).

Paul is saying that his calling to apostleship comes directly from Jesus Christ and God the Father. In other words, "These Judaizers are lying when they accuse me of being a self-appointed apostle."

In Paul's conversion story recorded in Acts 9:10-15, God tells a Christian leader, Ananias, to go to where Saul (later renamed Paul) is praying in Damascus, referring to Paul as "a chosen vessel."

The word "apostle" means "one who is sent forth." The term normally applies to missionaries, but it has a special meaning in the New Testament. It refers specifically to the 12 apostles of Jesus—as in Acts 1:21-22.

The case can be made that in reality Paul took the apostolic place of Judas. When the disciples chose Matthias, they did so before the outpouring of the Holy Spirit at Pentecost. They should have waited. If the Spirit had been allowed to guide fully in this matter, the apostles would have understood that God's choice was Saul of Tarsus—soon to be known as Paul.

In verse 2 Paul tells the Galatians that the "brethren" with him back up his apostleship. Significantly, he calls his coworkers "brethren," because the word "apostle" refers only to the select 12 chosen to be the pillars of the early Christian church. He calls them brethren. He does not call them apostles, though they are coworkers with him.

In verse 3 he wishes them "Grace and peace." This is the briefest greeting Paul ever uses in a New Testament epistle, and he moves immediately to a discussion of the gospel, writing in verse 4 that Jesus is the one who gave Himself for humanity's sins.

When Christ gave Himself, says Paul, He gave everything—as John says in 1 John 5:11, He gave His life. God gave His Son; Jesus gave Himself to deliver humanity from the present evil world. Why? Because the world stands condemned under the curse of God's law. But in Christ salvation is full and complete—there is nothing humanity can add to this salvation. Salvation is not partly by grace and partly by works. The moment anything is added to this gospel of grace, it becomes adulterated—perverted.

The Galatian Christians faced this serious issue. In Galatians 5:4 we will soon study Paul's statement that the moment law keeping is added as a requirement for justification, those who accept this polluted gospel fall from grace. A clear understanding of Galatians can help prevent us from falling into the same pit.

The Galatian Problem

With this in mind, let us turn to the Galatian problem, stated clearly in verses 6-10. Paul begins with the words "I marvel," in other words, "I am astonished, I am absolutely shocked." Why?

Because shortly before the Galatians had accepted the pure gospel with overwhelming support (see Galatians 4:15), but now they are deserting that gospel. The phrase "so soon removed" as in the King James Version can be misleading, since the Greek is not in the passive or in the past but in the present tense, active voice. Paul is saying here "you have already begun turning away from the gospel, so quickly."

If Paul is writing this letter to the Galatians from Corinth (which is distinctly possible), then the Galatians are turning away from the gospel only three years after having accepted it. But if this letter is being written from Ephesus (an equally possible scenario), then it has only been one year since they accepted the gospel.

Christians today face this same danger. The moment they accept Jesus Christ as their Savior and come under the umbrella of justification by faith alone, the devil begins working to sidetrack them.

By Grace Alone

The essence of Paul's gospel is salvation by grace alone. Ephesians 2:8, 9 expresses it clearly. "For by grace you have been saved through faith, and that not of yourselves; it is the gift of God." Paul says the same thing in 2 Corinthians 5:18 and again in Acts 20:24. Paul's is a message of grace alone.

But the Judaizers come with a different gospel—salvation by grace *plus* circumcision, *plus* keeping the law, *plus* good works.

In Galatians 1:7 Paul makes it clear that this perverts the true gospel: "There are some (*that is, the Judaizers*), who trouble you and would pervert the gospel of our Lord Jesus Christ."

The word "trouble" here actually refers to the Judaizers trying to "convince" the Christians by applying pressure. The Judaizers are fighters and manipulators, set on perverting the gospel of Jesus Christ. The word "pervert" is strong in the Greek, and rightly so. The Judaizers in effect are changing the gospel from good *news* to good *advice*, which in the end is bad news, if the advice proves impossible to follow.

But the gospel is much, much more than *good advice*. It is incredible good news. The good news is this—that in Jesus Christ God has obtained for mankind salvation full and complete.

Paul adds in Galatians 1:8, "But even if we (*the "we" refers to himself and his coworkers and most probably all the other apostles)* or an angel from heaven, preach any other gospel to you than that which we have preached to you, let him be accursed, let him be anathema."

Paul feels strongly about those who pervert the gospel and here uses very strong terms, "Let him be accursed." The word "accursed" or "anathema" refers to *eternal* loss, or damnation. "May God's wrath come upon such a person," Paul is saying, and verse 9 repeats the same thoughts, emphasizing the seriousness of tampering with the gospel.

Paul's final words in verse 10 clearly indicate that no Christian must ever be a man-pleaser but must please God. Christians serve Jesus Christ. He is their Lord and Master.

Galatianism

What is Galatianism, in a nutshell? It's anything that sidetracks human beings from the pure gospel. Paul's epistle is his reaction—his astonishment and righteous indignation—at how soon the Galatians could leave behind what they had once so eagerly embraced. The "we" and the "angel" he refers to can be anyone—you, me, a supernatural being—who tries to pervert the gospel.

The Galatians are in serious danger of losing their salvation by turning to a perverted gospel, and so it can happen today.

We must treat this epistle very seriously. Paul's strong words show that he is no man-pleaser but a faithful servant of God, and so Christians must be today. The devil has not stopped sidetracking Christians from the truth as it is in Christ, and so let us walk step by step through this epistle.

Galatians tells us that there is indeed only one gospel, for all time and all mankind. In Old Testament times and New Testament times, among Jews and Gentiles alike, that one gospel is the only one that can save mankind.

Some today say there are many roads to heaven—among them Christianity. Yet, the Bible tells us that there is only one Mediator between a holy God and sinful man and only one way to stand legally just before God's holy law. This comes only through faith in the doing and the dying of the Lord, Jesus Christ (1 Timothy 2:5-7). Salvation in all other religions is based on *do's* while Christianity is based on *done*.

The Judaizers had appeared once in Antioch to pervert the gospel, and Paul and Barnabas had taken the threat seriously. Acts 15 tells us exactly what took place and how Paul feels about anyone who tries to pervert the gospel.

We read that certain men came from Judea and taught the brethren, "Unless you are circumcised according to the custom of Moses, you cannot be saved." Paul was not against circumcision; he embraced good works and uplifted the law as a standard of Christian living. But the moment any of these three things become requirements for salvation, the gospel has been perverted.

So we read in Acts 15:2: "Therefore, when Paul and Barnabas had no small dissension and dispute with them, they determined that Paul and Barnabas and certain others of them should go up to Jerusalem to the apostles and elders about this question."

What a crucial moment in the history of the Christian church! Will the apostles agree with the apostle Paul? Thank God, the apostles in Jerusalem defend Paul, for we read in Acts 15:10: "Now, therefore, why do you test God by putting a yoke on the necks of the disciples which neither our fathers nor we were able to bear?"

Verse 11 continues: "But we believe (*that is, we apostles*) that through the grace of the Lord Jesus Christ we shall be saved in the same manner as they."

"We" refers to the Jews and "they" refers to the Gentiles. Mankind can be saved in one, and only one, way—through faith in the righteousness of Christ.

I pray that all Christians reading this book will never allow anyone to sidetrack them from the gospel. And to those who have not yet given themselves to Jesus Christ, my plea is that there is only one way to heaven—through faith in Jesus Christ and Him crucified. May the study of this important epistle lead us all to the Truth that sets us free (John 8:32, 36).

Chapter 2
Origin of Paul's Gospel
Galatians 1:11-24

Almost immediately after Paul established churches in Galatia, false teachers known as Judaizers infiltrated these churches and directed a powerful attack on Paul's apostolic authority and his gospel of salvation by grace alone. Galatians is Paul's response.

We looked last chapter at Galatians 1:1-10, where Paul introduces the Galatian problem. But he first presents himself in verses 1-5 as an apostle chosen by the authority of Jesus Christ and God the Father. Unlike Matthias, who was chosen by the other disciples to replace Judas, God the Father and Jesus Christ Himself have called Paul to be an apostle.

The Galatian Problem

In verses 6-10 Paul begins to take on the challenge of the Galatian Christians' problem. He is astonished that they are so soon turning their backs on the true gospel, which they had once received with great joy. Now they are accepting a perverted gospel that is stealing their joy and peace in Christ. Paul warns them that anyone—man or angel—who modifies or perverts the true gospel comes under the irrevocable curse of God.

Origin of Paul's Gospel

The problem Paul faces with the Galatians remains with us today in all Christian denominations. How important, then, that we come to grips with Paul's message. As we study the concluding verses of Chapter 1, we discover how Paul deals with the Judaizers' second attack—this one on the origin of his gospel.

In Galatians 1:11-24 Paul tells us that just as his apostolic authority comes directly from God, so his gospel of grace alone is a product of direct revelation from Jesus Christ Himself.

In Galatians 1:11,12 Paul reminds the Galatians: "But I make known to you, brethren, that the gospel which was preached by me, is not according to man. For I neither received it from man, nor was I taught it, but it came through the revelation of Jesus Christ."

In verses 6-10 Paul has already said there is only one gospel—that the gospel is the measuring-stick by which all human teaching is tested. This one gospel is not a human invention or philosophy. It comes by direct revelation of Jesus Christ—as directly as the other 11 apostles received it from Jesus during His three-year earthly ministry.

In verses 13-24, then, Paul gives a detailed account of how this occurred, and in verses 20-24 he presents the history of his post-conversion learning experience: "For you have heard of my former conduct in Judaism, how I persecuted the church of God beyond measure and tried to destroy it. And I advanced in Judaism beyond many of my contemporaries in my own nation, being more exceedingly zealous for the traditions of my fathers. But when it pleased God, who separated me from my mother's womb and called me through his grace, to reveal his Son to me, that I might preach Him among the Gentiles, I did not immediately confer with flesh and blood, nor did I go up to Jerusalem to those who were apostles before me; but I went to Arabia, and returned again to Damascus. Then after three years I went up to Jerusalem to see Peter, and remained with him fifteen days. But I saw none of the other apostles, except James, the Lord's brother. (Now concerning the things which I write to you, indeed, before God, I do not lie.) Afterward, I went into the regions of Syria and Cilicia and I was unknown by face to the churches of Judea which were in Christ. But they were hearing only, he who formerly persecuted us now preaches the faith, which he once tried to destroy. And they glorified God in me."

Paul reminds the Galatian Christians in verse 13 that he was once a persecutor of the Christian faith (see also Acts 8:1-3; 9:1, 2). In Philippians 3:6 Paul explains what kind of man he was as a Pharisee. He tells the Galatians that as a Jew he had been enjoying great success and had no reason, humanly speaking, for giving it up. But God Himself intervened.

God's Initiative

God Himself took the initiative to lead Paul from Judaism to Christianity, says Galatians 1:15: "But when it pleased God, who separated me from my mother's womb and called me to His grace. . . ."

This is true not only of Paul's history but of every believer's. God takes the initiative; He is the One who comes with the wonderful news of the gospel. By nature we flee from God, for we are sinners. We are afraid of God, but He comes to us through the gospel and says, "Stop running away from Me. I have not come to destroy you. I have come to bring you good news."

God called Paul by grace. Grace means undeserved merit. In 1 Corinthians 15:9 Paul refers to himself as the least of the apostles, adding in so many words: "I don't deserve to be an apostle, because I persecuted the Christian church." But God called Paul because Paul's heart was right. Paul believed that in persecuting the Christian church he was serving God and he brings this out clearly in Philippians 3:4-6. Because God knew that Paul was honest, God took the initiative and revealed His beloved Son to Paul.

"God appointed me as an apostle, as a missionary to you Gentiles," Paul is saying in Galatians 1:16: "To reveal His Son in me, that I might preach Him among the Gentiles; immediately I conferred not with flesh and blood (*I did not go to the apostles or to some human agent to find out what this gospel is all about*)."

Paul did not question God's calling. He did not consult with any man but went straight to Arabia. The word "Arabia" here refers to an area just south of Damascus, so Paul did not have to travel a great distance to get there.

In verse 18 Paul says: "After three years. . . . (*that is, three years after his conversion).*" Many believe that those three years in Arabia correspond to the three-year period of instruction Jesus gave His other apostles during His earthly mission.

Paul is saying here that after these three years—that is, three years after his conversion—he finally travels to Jerusalem, where he sees Peter. But the visit is a fairly short one—only for 15 days. Why does Paul mention the number of days? Because he wants his readers to know that it would have been impossible in those 15 days for Peter to have given him the full counsel of God that he has proclaimed to the Galatian Christians. In other words, "I could not have received this message from Peter."

He also briefly visited James but saw none of the other apostles. Again Paul emphasizes that he had no opportunity to be taught the message of the gospel from any man—only from Christ Himself.

What did Paul do during those three years in Arabia? First, he restudied the Old Testament in light of Jesus Christ. As a Pharisee, Paul knew the Old Testament inside out, but he had misunderstood its message. In those three years Christ did for Paul what He had done for the two Christians on the road to Emmaus, soon after His resurrection.

Like Paul on the road to Damascus, the two men met Jesus but at first did not know who He was. They believed that Jesus was dead, but Jesus chided them (as He did Paul), "You are so slow to learn the truth" (Luke 24:25).

Jesus began with the story of Moses and presented an eye-opening overview of Scriptures and prophecy that pointed to Him as the Messiah (see also Luke 24:27).

During Paul's three years in Arabia, God likewise opened to Paul the true meaning of the Old Testament as a prophetic precursor of Jesus Christ.

After Three Years. . .

After three years Paul's gospel is fully formulated through the abundant revelation God has given him. Armed with the full gospel, then, Paul returns to Jerusalem to visit briefly (Galatians 1:18-20) with the apostles Peter and James.

In verse 21 Paul now says that after visiting Peter and James, "I went to the regions of Syria and Cilicia." This is an area near Tyre and Sidon, in ancient Phoenicia, and Paul here is pointing out that he had no opportunity to visit the Judean Christians: "I was unknown by face to the churches of Judea which were in Christ."

The Judean Christians knew Paul only as a persecutor, but news had reached them that this former persecutor had made a complete turnaround and was now preaching the message of salvation in Christ.

What did the Judean Christians do with this news? "They glorified God in me," Paul says, though the Judaizers continued to oppose him.

Chapter 1 in a Nutshell

What does Galatians 1 tell us in a nutshell? First, Paul makes it clear that he is neither a self-appointed apostle nor chosen by a committee or dignitary of the early Christian church. He is an apostle called by Jesus Christ and God the Father as a chosen vessel.

Paul is not defending his personal right to apostleship. He defends his apostleship only as a means of defeating the Judaizers; Paul legitimizes his apostleship only to enable him more persuasively to defend the pure gospel God has given him to preach.

Second, Paul is astonished. He is shocked that the Galatian Christians are so soon sidetracked from the true gospel. When we come to chapter four, we will find that the Galatians were initially so grateful for the gospel of salvation by grace alone that they were willing to pluck out their own eyes and give them to Paul, who was having problems with his eyes at that time.

But now, within three years and perhaps as little as one year, they are turning their backs on the message of salvation by grace alone. Why do human beings so readily turn their backs on the gospel? There are two reasons.

First, we are by nature legalists; we are inclined to believe, to teach, and to practice salvation by works because our sinful natures earnestly want to live independently of God.

The second reason is that the gospel offers salvation by grace alone. It allows for no human contribution to salvation, and this presents a tremendous blow to the egocentric nature that wants to take part, if not full credit for saving itself. The gospel throws any glory of man in the dust.

Accepting the gospel calls on us to admit the painful truth that we are spiritually bankrupt. Our egocentric nature revels at the thoughts that it may be possible for us to contribute to our own salvation! No wonder the Galatians are so easily deceived by the Judaizers.

We can imagine a discussion something like this: The Judaizers arrive in Galatia and say to the Christians, "We hear that you have been converted by the apostle Paul!"

"Yes!" the Galatians respond. "Paul came with a wonderful message of salvation, and we are rejoicing in it!"

The Judaizers respond, "Yes, we thank God that you have accepted Jesus Christ as your Savior. But you need to understand that what Paul preaches is not the complete story."

"Really!" the Galatians reply, "We thought Paul gave us the full counsel of God."

"Oh, no," reply the Judaizers. "What he told you is true, but incomplete. Surely you don't expect to go to heaven simply by believing in Jesus Christ. That's too good to be true! Friends, God expects you to show yourselves worthy of salvation. First, He expects you to be circumcised—as He did of Abraham. Second, He expects to see good works from you before you can be saved. And finally, He expects you to keep the law of Moses. Otherwise you will never make it to heaven."

The poor Galatian Christians are enticed and deceived by this perverted gospel, and Paul is astonished that they are so easily sidetracked.

The Galatians' failure is by no means unique to them; Christians today can fall into the same trap. This makes our careful study of Galatians vitally important, for it can help defend us from the terrible enemy of the gospel.

Final Summary

Paul tells us in Chapter 1 that he is an apostle by divine selection and as such he is amazed by the Galatians' rapid departure from the pure gospel. These are his first two major points.

Paul's third and final main point is that the gospel he preaches comes from Jesus Christ Himself, not from any man. "The day you refuse to accept the gospel that I give you, you are refusing not my message but the message of Jesus Christ Himself," Paul is saying. "This is a serious matter indeed."

If the message Paul preaches is simply his own idea, there is no danger in turning away from it. But if it comes directly from Jesus Christ, it becomes a different matter altogether.

Paul tells us that the gospel is, first of all, unchanging. Paul, Peter, and the other apostles all preach the same gospel. The emphasis and style may vary, as they address various audiences from various personal points of view, but the substance of the message is identical.

Second, to maintain the purity of the gospel is a sacred duty. The devil has not taken a vacation. He is eager to pervert the gospel of the Lord, Jesus Christ, and he uses any means possible. In today's world, he uses humanism, the New Age movement, and other forms of "new truth" to pervert it.

Adulterating the gospel is one of Satan's most powerful ways to pull men and women out of Christ. Paul writes in 2 Corinthians 11:3 and 4 that just as Satan deceived Eve, he will try and deceive the Corinthians through craft. Satan, the father of lies, is still alive today and can and will come as an angel of light and try to pervert the gospel in our lives (see 2 Corinthians 11:13-15).

Clearly Paul is an apostle of Jesus Christ. How important, then, that we study his writings, which make up almost half of the New Testament.

When Jesus came to this world, He came primarily to live and die for the sins of the world—to *be* the gospel. But he set aside Paul to explain the gospel. Paul is the theologian of the New Testament (Ephesians 3:8).

That theology came to him from Christ Himself, by revelation. In 2 Corinthians 12:7 and onward, Paul writes that because of the abundance of revelation—and with it the danger of pride infiltrating his heart—that God has allowed Satan to put a thorn in his flesh to keep him humble.

As we study this Epistle to the Galatians, my prayer is that all Christians who read will be rooted and grounded in the truth, as it is in Christ, and that nothing will sidetrack them.

Only one gospel can reconcile a holy God to sinful man—the gospel of the Lord, Jesus Christ. May none who have accepted this pure gospel ever turn aside to anything else in their Christian walk.

Chapter 3
Only One Gospel
Galatians 2:1-10

Though we have already studied the major points of Galatians 1, before moving forward to Galatians 2, let us briefly review.

Galatians 1 shows emphatically that Paul is ordained by God to be an apostle to the Gentiles. But wherever Paul goes, Jewish Christians who oppose his message dog his footsteps, troubling the new believers by telling them that to be saved they must be circumcised, do good works, and keep the law.

These "Judaizers" meet with considerable success. Even today, most Islamic scholars consider Paul and his message of salvation by grace to be the most heretical aspects of the Christian faith.

All religious movements that seek to promote legalism as an aspect of faith tend to hold Paul and his writings in low regard. Galatians 1 tells us that this disregard begins during Paul's lifetime itself, as the Judaizers launch their powerful two-pronged attack. They accuse Paul of being a self-appointed apostle and of inventing his own gospel.

But the Judaizers carry things a step further. They also try to put a wedge between Paul and the other apostles. They hint to the Gentile believers that the gospel Paul preaches is quite different from the one Peter and the other apostles are preaching in Palestine.

Since the Gentiles are in no position to test the truth of these insinuations, Paul begins to set the record straight in Chapter 1, proving that he and the other apostles are all preaching the same gospel.

Paul's Second Jerusalem Visit

This is the setting for Galatians 2:1-10, which reads: "Then after fourteen years I went up again to Jerusalem with Barnabas, and also took Titus with me. And I went up by revelation, and communicated to them that gospel which I preach among the Gentiles, but privately to those who were of reputation, lest by any means I might run, or had run, in vain. Yet not even Titus who was with me, being a Greek, was compelled to be circumcised. But this occurred because of false brethren secretly brought in (who came in by stealth to spy out our liberty which we have in Christ Jesus, that they might bring us into bondage), to whom we did not yield submission even for an hour, that the truth of the gospel might continue with you. But from those who seemed to be something—whatever they were, it makes no difference to me; God shows personal favoritism to no man—for those who seemed to be something added nothing to me. But on the contrary, when they saw that the gospel for the uncircumcised had been committed to me, as the gospel for the circumcised was to Peter (for he who worked effectively in Peter for the apostleship to the circumcised also worked effectively in me towards the Gentiles). And when James, Cephas and John who seemed to be pillars, perceived the grace that had been given to me, they gave me and Barnabas the right hand of fellowship, that we should go to the Gentiles and they to the circumcised. They desired only that we should remember the poor, the very thing that I also was eager to do."

The opening statement reads, "Then after fourteen years. . . ." Fourteen years after what? Fourteen years after his conversion, Paul again goes up to Jerusalem.

But this time he does not go alone. With him are Barnabas, a fellow Jew, and Titus, a Greek convert who is learning the ministry from Paul—we might call him an "intern" today.

Paul says they go up to Jerusalem "by revelation", not by

summons from the other apostles. God directs Paul to go of his own accord to Jerusalem. Why? Because of the damage the Judaizers are doing by their false teachings, telling Gentile believers that there is a discrepancy between the gospel Paul preaches and the gospel being taught by Peter, James, and John in Jerusalem.

God wants to put an end to this problem, and Paul says, "I went up by revelation, and communicated to them that gospel which I preached among the Gentiles."

In Jerusalem he shares with the other apostles the message that he has been proclaiming to the Gentiles. He does so privately with those of reputation—men identified in verse nine as James, Cephas (Peter), and John.

Paul writes, "I did it lest by any means I might run or had run in vain." Paul has no doubts about his gospel, but he wants to report to the leaders so that they may all be in perfect unity regarding the gospel they are all proclaiming.

This unity should be the goal of Christians today. The Christian church should preach only one gospel, and this epistle can help us come together in harmony on this question.

Paul now writes in verse 3: "Yet not even Titus who was with me, being a Greek, was compelled to be circumcised."

To understand this, we must keep in mind that the Judaizers are insisting that the Gentiles be circumcised. This is the central issue at the first Jerusalem council, which had taken place not long before Paul's second visit to Jerusalem and is recorded in Acts 15.

Paul is saying here that if what the Judaizers are saying is correct (that circumcision is essential for salvation), surely the brethren in Jerusalem would have required Titus, a Gentile minister, to be circumcised. Titus was a test case. The whole unity of the gospel depended on how the pillars of the Christian church in Jerusalem responded to Titus.

Paul says in verse 4, "But this occurred because of false brethren secretly brought in (*the Judaizers*) who came to spy on the liberty which we have in Christ, that they might bring us into bondage."

The "we" here refers to Paul and the other apostles. If the Judaizers had succeeded in bringing a wedge between Paul and the other apostles, the Christian church might not have lasted long. But Paul was able to prove that the apostles were perfectly united in their stand.

Paul adds in verse 5: "To whom we (*Paul and the other apostles, Peter, James, and John*) did not yield submission even for an hour, that the truth of the gospel might continue with you." Not for a single moment did the apostles allow the Judaizers to pervert the gospel or bring a wedge between them.

Perfect Harmony

Today the Christian church is fragmented by many issues, but on one thing all must be clear—the church must be united when it comes to defining the gospel of Jesus Christ.

Paul continues, "But from those who seem to be something—whatever they were, it makes no difference to me. . . ." Paul is not being disrespectful to the leaders and believers in Jerusalem, only reminding them of the priesthood of all believers—that God shows personal favoritism to no man, for we all, apostles and laity, leaders and members of the church, are 100 percent sinners, saved by grace. There is no distinction under the umbrella of the gospel of the Lord, Jesus Christ (Galatians 3:27, 28).

Then Paul says a wonderful thing in verse six: "For those who seem to be something added nothing to me."

The leading brethren in Jerusalem do not contradict, add to, modify, or supplement Paul's gospel. They concur that Paul's message is full and complete—salvation for all mankind comes only by the grace of the Lord, Jesus Christ,

Paul then continues in verse 7, "But on the contrary, when they saw that the gospel for the uncircumcised (*the Gentiles*) had been committed to me, as the gospel for the circumcised (*the Jews*) was to Peter (for he who worked effectively in Peter for the apostleship to the circumcised also worked effectively in me towards the Gentiles)."

Jesus Christ is the Source of the gospel. The gospel proclaimed by Peter to the Jews and by Paul to the Gentiles is the same gospel. There is no distinction. Paul and Peter preach the same gospel. True, they are speaking to different audiences, and their styles therefore may differ; their approaches are distinctive. But the message is one.

Paul says in verse 9: "And when James, Cephas, and John who seemed to be pillars (*the leading brethren of God's church in Jerusalem*), perceived the grace that had been given to me, they gave me and Barnabas the right hand of fellowship."

These apostles say to Paul and Barnabas, in other words, "Continue the good work. We are perfectly united." What a crucial moment in the history of the Christian church. It shows that the Judaizers are liars and deceivers—agents of Satan who want to destroy the truth as it is in Christ. Before Paul and Barnabas leave Jerusalem, they establish beyond a doubt that the message they all preach is one and the same. The Jerusalem brethren desire but one thing, Paul says in verse 10—that the Gentile believers remember Jewish believers who are being persecuted and facing financial and material hardships.

Paul says, "I was fully aware of this and I was eager to help the believers in Jerusalem wherever I have proclaimed the gospel."

Two Important Facts

We must remember two important facts concerning the message of Galatians 2:1-10. First, the truth of the gospel is unchanging. Paul says in Galatians 1:8 and 9 that anyone who brings a gospel other than the one he and the other apostles preach are accursed of God—though that person be an angel from heaven.

Peter, Paul, and the other apostles are perfectly united on how mankind is justified before God. The same should apply to the church today.

Yes, emphasis and style may vary. For example, Paul's greatest enemies in his proclamation of the gospel are the Judaizers—and legalism. So Paul in his writings speaks a great deal against legalism (salvation by works of the law).

In writing to Jewish believers, however, James deals with an opposite problem—"cheap grace", or antinomianism. Both were preaching the same gospel in perfect harmony, but they were dealing with two different problems—two distinctive groups of people. So their approaches differ.

The second truth we must remember is that the purity of the gospel must be maintained at all costs. Perverting the gospel is one of Satan's favorite ways of destroying believers' faith and unity. Paul says in Galatians 5:3 and 4 that anyone who adds law-keeping to justification by faith alone in the righteousness of Christ has fallen from grace and makes Christ of no value. All through his ministry Paul warned his believers to be on guard against perverting the gospel.

In 2 Corinthians 4:3, for example, Paul writes, "But even if our gospel is veiled, it is veiled to those who are perishing, whose minds the god of this age has blinded, who do not believe, lest the light of the gospel of the glory of Christ, who is the image of God, should shine on them."

The devil to a large degree has put a veil in front of the eyes of many of today's Christians. He convinces them that man has within himself the power to save himself: I must do my best and Christ will make up the rest.

Karl Marx's Mistake

Interestingly enough, Karl Marx made this mistake—a mistake many who believe in humanism continue to make. But the Bible says clearly that no one can save himself from sin by his own good works, for sin is not only an act that condemns us but a slavery; sin is a law (constant force) that dwells within and cannot produce holy living (Romans 7:14-25).

Later in our study, we will find in Galatians 3:10 that all who depend on the law for their salvation fall under a curse, for no human being has been able to obey the law perfectly and continually.

In 2 Corinthians 11:3 and 4 Paul says, "But I fear lest somehow as the serpent deceived Eve by his craftiness, so your minds may be corrupted from the simplicity that is in Christ. For if he who comes preaches another Jesus whom we have not preached, or if you receive a different spirit which you have not received, or a different gospel which you have not accepted, you may well put up with it."

In other words Paul is saying, "I am concerned for you Corinthian Christians. It is so easy to sidetrack you from the true gospel," and this is true of all Christians today. Legalism is very appealing to the egocentric nature. But the gospel is a standard that shows us how spiritually poverty-stricken we are. How important that Christians maintain the purity of the gospel—that none be allowed to pervert the gospel, as the devil has been trying to do from the beginning.

Paul clearly refers back to the Jerusalem Council in Galatians 2, for the language of Galatians 2:1-10 and Acts 15: 6-11 are particularly similar. The issue in both is whether circumcision and keeping the law are requirements for salvation. The apostles at the Jerusalem Council "came together to consider this matter (*that is, are circumcision and law-keeping a requirement for salvation?*) And when there had been much dispute, Peter (*a pillar of the church*) rose up and said to them (*the congregation*), 'Men and brethren, you know that a good while ago God chose among us, that by my mouth the Gentiles should hear the word of the gospel and believe. So God, who knows the heart, acknowledged them, by giving them the Holy Spirit just as He did to us, and made no distinction between us and them, purifying their hearts by faith. Now therefore, why do you (*"you" primarily refers to the Judaizers*) test God by putting a yoke on the necks of the disciples (*the believers*) which neither our fathers nor we were able to bear?'"

Same Gospel, Same Salvation

Peter is reminding the Judaizers that Judaism for 1,500 years had miserably failed to produce the kind of righteousness that could stand before the judgment seat of God (see Romans 9:30-32).

In Acts 15:11 we read: "But we believe that through the grace of the Lord Jesus Christ we shall be saved in the same manner as they." In other words God saves mankind in only one way. Whether Jew or a Gentile, male or female, educated or uneducated, first-world or third-world born, sinful man can be justified in only one way before a holy God—through grace by faith and not of works (Ephesians 2:8,9).

May this truth set us all free, and may none sidetrack us from this gospel of grace alone. We can thank God for Paul and his Epistle to the Galatians, for the truth in Jesus Christ he champions in this letter can truly set us free.

Chapter 4
Justification by Faith Alone

Galatians 2:11-21

Paul has just described his second visit to Jerusalem, 14 years after his conversion. There he proves conclusively that the gospel he preaches to the Gentiles is identical to the gospel that apostles Peter, James, and John have been preaching in Jerusalem.

In Galatians 2:11-21 the scene changes from Jerusalem, the Jewish nation's capital, to Antioch, chief city of Syria. Here Paul describes his clash with Peter, one of the most dramatic episodes in the New Testament, as two leading apostles of Jesus Christ face off on a matter of principle.

Paul and Peter Disagree

What prompts Paul to publicly oppose Peter? Has he lost his temper or is he threatened by Peter's presence? Is Paul trying to contain Peter's power, as one presidential candidate tries to appear more charismatic than his opponent? Or is Paul jealous?

As we might expect, the controversy between these two leaders is anything but mundane. But before we consider the issues involved in Galatians 2:11-21, let us recognize four indisputable facts: Both Paul and Peter are born-again Christians; both are genuine apostles of Jesus Christ; God is mightily using both (The Book of Acts, in its first half describes how God used Peter mightily; the second half focuses on God's mighty leading of Paul's ministry); and, both men play a leading role in establishing the Christian church.

Yet here we find them in open conflict.

Verses 11-16 tell the story in Galatians 2: "But when Peter had come to Antioch, I withstood him to his face, because he was to be blamed; for before certain men came from James, he would eat with the Gentiles; but when they came, he withdrew and separated himself, fearing those who were of the circumcision. And the rest of the Jews also played the hypocrite with him, so that even Barnabas was carried away with their hypocrisy. But when I saw that they were not straightforward about the truth of the gospel, I said to Peter before them all, 'If you, being a Jew, live with the manner of Gentiles and not as the Jews, why do you compel Gentiles to live as Jews? We who are Jews by nature, and not sinners of the Gentiles, knowing that a man is not justified by the works of the law but by faith in Jesus Christ, even we have believed in Christ Jesus, that we might be justified by faith in Christ and not by the works of the law; For by the works of the law no flesh shall be justified.'"

Paul first identifies the place and occasion: "But when Peter had come to Antioch. . . ." Antioch is the chief Syrian city in Paul's time—an important place, both in the commercial and Christian world, for here believers were first called "Christians."

Why then does Paul rebuke Peter? The answer is found in verse 12. Before the Judaizers (Jewish Christians zealous to impose Jewish law on the Gentiles) arrive in Antioch, Peter openly eats with Gentiles. But when these critical Jewish Christians come to Antioch, he withdraws completely from the company of Gentiles and eats only with Jews, perhaps fearing the wrath of his Jewish brethren back in Jerusalem.

To fully understand verse 12 we must remember that in the early church, members often gather to eat a meal together in an *agape* (ah-GAH-pay) feast.

For many Christian slaves, this meal is the best of the week, shared by Jews and Gentile Christians, slaves and masters. Yet, such *agape* meals are completely alien to the Jews' culture at that time, which strictly forbids such socializing. A Jew cannot travel with *Gentiles* or share his meals or accommodations. The gospel, however, has liberated Christian Jews from these restrictive attitudes. In Ephesians 2:14-18 Paul says that Jesus Christ, by His death on the cross, has broken down the partition that separated Jews and the Gentiles in the Jerusalem temple. There is now no barrier between them, and in Galatians 3:28 Paul says, "There is neither Jew nor Greek (*Gentiles*), there is neither slave nor free, there is neither male nor female for you all are one in Christ Jesus." What a wonderful privilege to belong to a church that makes no such distinctions!

Peter too practiced separatism, until God bade him change his behavior. Acts 10:9-23 tells the story of how one day Peter falls asleep on his house roof as he waits for his noon meal to be served. While he sleeps he dreams that all kinds of ceremonially unclean animals descend from heaven in a net and that a voice tells him to slay these animals and eat them.

In the dream Peter protests, "I have never eaten anything unclean." But the same voice reprimands him, "Peter, what God has cleansed you must not call common."

Peter immediately senses that this is no ordinary dream and that God is using the unclean animals to teach him that he should never again consider Gentiles unclean.

Peter abandons separatism and at the Jerusalem Council cited in Acts 15, Peter declares that there is no distinction in the eyes of God between Jews and Gentiles.

But now a group of Jewish brethren have appeared on the scene in Antioch, claiming to have been sent by James, leader of the Christian church in Jerusalem. Their claim is questionable, but trouble begins when Peter begins eating only with Jews, "fearing those who were of the circumcision."

Peter is clearly not infallible and is now setting a terrible example for the Antioch church.

This is why Paul openly rebukes him, for all the Jewish Christians are beginning to imitate Peter's example, including

Barnabas. They are practicing what Paul calls hypocrisy. Peter, not by conviction but by behavior, is giving the impression that he regards the Gentiles as "unclean." His behavior is at complete odds with the gospel of His Lord.

So Paul writes in Galatians 2:14: "But when I saw that they were not straightforward about the truth of the gospel. . . ." By "they" Paul means Peter and the other Jews, including Barnabas, Paul's co-laborer. Barnabas had fought the Judaizers in the Jerusalem Council, but now has succumbed to pressure from Jerusalem.

In his rebuke to Peter in the second half of verse 14, Paul says: "If you, being a Jew, live in the manner of Gentiles and not as the Jews, why do you compel Gentiles to live as Jews?"

To understand Paul's reasoning we must put ourselves in the Jewish culture. The Jews believe they should not associate with Gentiles, for the Gentiles are spiritually inferior. But when Peter began to eat with the Gentiles, he admitted two things—first, that like the Gentiles, he is a sinner himself, and second, that like any Gentile, he is saved by grace alone.

Peter's non-separatist behavior represented the gospel truth that in God's eyes there is no distinction between Jew and Gentile. All have sinned (Romans 3:23) and come short of the glory of God, and both are justified freely by the grace of the Lord, Jesus Christ.

But when Peter separates himself from the Gentiles, he is implying that the Gentiles are again "unclean." He seems to be agreeing with the Jewish Christians who have come from Jerusalem.

In doing so Peter is contradicting the very stand he took at the Jerusalem Council. Paul reminds him in verse 16, "knowing that a man is not justified by the works of the law but by faith in Jesus Christ. Even we (*"we" refers to the Jews*) have believed in Christ Jesus that we (*Jews*) might be justified by faith in Christ and not by the works of the law, for by the works of the law no flesh (*Jews or Gentiles*) shall be justified."

Paul is saying, "Peter, you know the truth; you defended it in the Jerusalem Council. Now why do you contradict that truth by leaving the Gentiles' table and going only to the Jews'?"

He adds more food for thought in verses 17-21: "But if, while we seek to be justified by Christ, we ourselves also are found sinners, is Christ therefore, a minister of sin? Certainly not! For if I build again those things which I destroyed; I make myself a transgressor. For I through the law died to the law that I might live to God. I have been crucified with Christ; it is no longer I who live, but Christ lives in me; and the life which I now live in the flesh I live by faith in the Son of God, who loved me and gave Himself for me. I do not set aside the grace of God; for if righteousness comes through the law, then Christ died in vain."

Justification

What a precious message! In verse 16 Paul sums up for Peter the fundamental truth of the gospel and provides a summary passage for the whole epistle. Paul's central thrust in this letter is clearly that justification is by faith alone—and nothing else.

An important word has appeared here for the first time in Galatians—a word central to the message of God, central to the gospel Paul preaches, and central to Christianity itself. Nobody truly understands Christianity who does not understand this word—the word "justified."

It appears in verb form three times in verse 16 and once in verse 17. Its noun form, "Justification", appears once in verse 21.

Since verse 16 is key to this epistle, let us read it once again and carefully search out its full significance: "Knowing that a man is not justified by the works of the law but by faith in Jesus Christ. Even we have believed in Christ Jesus that we might be justified by faith in Christ and not by the works of the law, for by the works of the law no flesh shall be justified."

The first words, "Knowing that a man is not justified by the works of the law. . . ." tell us that Peter already understands what Paul is saying. "You yourself declared that we are justified by faith apart from the works of the law, at the Jerusalem Council," Paul essentially reminds him.

But what does this word "justified" mean?

First, we know it to be a legal term, and in Deuteronomy 25:1 we find it used in that legal sense, "If there is a dispute between men, and they come to court, that the judges may judge them, and they justify the righteous and condemn the wicked." By definition, the law can only justify those who *keep* the law. For 1,500 years the Jews have tried to justify themselves by the works of the law (Paul uses "works of the law" to mean "legalism." There is no Greek word in his day equivalent to the English word "legalism.")

The Jews, who try to justify themselves by the works of the law, have failed miserably. Paul brings this out clearly in Romans 9:30-33. Peter knows this. Yet what Peter does in refusing to eat with the Gentiles flatly contradicts his belief.

Many Christians limit the word "justified" to forgiveness. True, a sinner must receive forgiveness of his sins. But justification in the New Testament sense means more than forgiveness—wonderful as forgiveness is—because forgiveness simply means that one's sins have been canceled.

Justification by faith as preached by Paul, however, includes more than this. Paul brings this out in Romans 5:18: "By the obedience of one (*Jesus Christ*), justification unto life was brought to all men."

Justification to life requires not only forgiveness but positive righteousness. To be justified before God's holy law, two things are required: perfect obedience and perfect justice. Only in Christ can sinners possess perfect obedience and perfect justice. Apart from Christ, Paul says, sinners cannot possibly be justified before God.

Paul's words in Galatians 2:17 may seem confusing at first: "But if while we seek to be justified by Christ, we ourselves also are found sinners. Is Christ therefore a minister of sin? Certainly not!"

The text seems confusing because it could mean two things—both equally valid. Paul may indeed be referring to the ethical issue of whether to eat with Gentiles. Peter has already acknowledged that Gentiles and Jews are equal before Christ. But by his cowardly act, Peter implies that Gentile believers are still *unclean*. If indeed Gentiles are unclean, Peter is making Christ (who justifies Gentiles by faith) a minister of sin.

Cheap Grace

But Paul may be actually be referring to what we know today as *cheap grace*. The Judaizers, who oppose Paul's gospel of grace, include the keeping of the law as a requirement for salvation. They insist that if sin-prone human beings are justified by faith alone, the door opens for what theologians term antinomianism, or cheap grace.

In other words, a new convert might say, "Since I am already justified by faith in the perfect history of Jesus Christ that took place 2,000 years ago, I can say with Paul in Romans 6:1 that I will 'keep on sinning that grace may abound.'" The Judaizers argue that Paul's teachings lead directly to such behavior.

Paul may have both meanings in mind. He answers that such behavior (in both the ethical and cheap grace scenarios) is "unthinkable." Verses 19 and 20 explain Paul's application of the gospel to the justified believer: "For I through the law died to the law that I might live to God." Paul is saying two things in verse 19: First he tells us that as far as the law is concerned, he is dead.

Paul knows (see Romans 7:1) that the law has dominion over human beings only as long as they are alive. The moment they accept death in Christ, the law no longer has dominion over them.

But Christ does not set His followers free from the law so that they can live as they please. He sets them free to live unto God. Paul brings this out in Galatians 2:20: "I have been crucified with Christ (*It is there that I was redeemed from under law*): It is no longer I who live but Christ lives in me and the life which I now live in the flesh, I live by faith in the Son of God who loved me and gave Himself for me."

Justification by faith means the believer can say, "I am crucified with Christ. It is no longer I but Christ who must live in me."

True justification by faith says, "Not I, but Christ." And since Christ is the same yesterday, today, and forever, the life He lives in the believer will be the life He lived 2,000 years ago—a life of righteousness, a life going about doing good.

This is genuine justification by faith. What Christ does in the Christian does not contribute to his or her salvation; Christians are justified by faith alone in the perfect history of Christ, but the fruits of justification by faith are holy living.

Paul brings this out clearly in Romans 6, especially verse 22: "But now having been set free from sin, and having become slaves to God, you have your fruit to holiness and the end, everlasting life."

Paul concludes Galatians 2:21 with these words: "I do not set aside the grace of God; for if righteousness comes through the law, then Christ died in vain."

On one hand Christians are justified by faith alone in the righteousness of Christ. What Christians do—even what the Holy Spirit does in them—contributes nothing to their justification. On the other hand, a justified Christian will always say, "I have been crucified with Christ; it is no longer I who live but the life I now live is Christ living in me through faith in Him who loved me and gave Himself for me."

This is Paul's balanced message. Christ's followers are

always justified by faith in the doing and dying of Christ—nothing else. But the wonderful truth that sets the Christian free produces a life of holiness.

Chapter 5
O Foolish Galatians

Galatians 3:1-9

The apostle Paul in Galatians 1 and 2 strongly defends the divine origin of his apostolic calling and the gospel of grace he preaches.

Now in Galatians 3 he turns his attention to the Galatians' own experience as they first responded to the gospel message. Let us read Galatians 3:1-9: "Oh, foolish Galatians! Who has bewitched you that you should not obey the truth, before whose eyes Jesus Christ was clearly portrayed among you as crucified? This only I want to learn from you: Did you receive the Spirit by the works of the law, or by the hearing of faith? Are you so foolish? Having begun in the Spirit, are you now being made perfect by the flesh? Have you suffered so many things in vain—if indeed it was in vain? Therefore, he who supplies the Spirit to you and works miracles among you, does he do it by the works of the law, or by the hearing of faith? 'Just as Abraham believed God, and it was accounted to him for righteousness.' Therefore know that only those who are of faith are sons of Abraham. And the Scripture, foreseeing that God would justify the Gentiles by faith, preached the gospel to Abraham beforehand, saying, 'In you all the nations shall be blessed.' So then those who are of faith, are blessed with believing Abraham."

Foolish Questions

This passage is divided into two parts: Notice that verses 1-5 deal with the past experience of the Galatian Christians, posed as a series of questions; in verses 6-9, however, Paul speaks of Abraham, the father of all who believe. He uses

Abraham as an example—a prototype—of how the gospel saves individual believers.

Paul begins the passage with a very strong statement: "Oh, foolish Galatians." The word "foolish" means "unthinking" or "idiotic", implying irrational behavior or stupidity. If Paul were writing today he would say, "You *stupid, idiotic* Galatians." Any Christian who turns from the glorious gospel of salvation by grace alone and desires to be saved by personal good works truly deserves to be called foolish—for what he or she is doing is pure stupidity.

The Galatians are acting like a group of farmers who decide to park their tractors and plow with oxen. Their behavior is so irrational that Paul wonders if someone has cast a spell on them: "Who has bewitched you (*who has cast a spell on you*)?"

Paul uses the word "who" in the *singular*—though the Judaizers are a *group* of people. Clearly Paul is suggesting that the enemy of souls—Satan—is the real culprit behind the Galatians' foolish behavior.

In 2 Corinthians 11:3 and 4 Paul says that just as the serpent beguiled Eve, Satan can lead believers to accept a false gospel.

The Galatians have been deceived into turning their backs on their only hope of salvation—Jesus Christ and Him crucified. But Paul isn't finished with them yet; he probes further: "Tell me, you who obeyed the truth, did you obey the fact that Jesus Christ was portrayed before you crucified?"

Preaching Christ Crucified

Paul preaches a message of Jesus Christ and Him crucified as man's only hope. In 1 Corinthians 1:17 and 18 he identifies the cross of Christ with the gospel, the power of God unto salvation. Such a message is foolishness to the world, but to those who believe, the cross is the power of God unto salvation.

Paul says in 1 Corinthians 2:1 and 2 that when preaching in

Corinth he emphasized Jesus Christ and Him crucified: "I wanted to know nothing else among you when I came to you, except Jesus Christ and Him crucified." This is the heart of the gospel message. Man's redemption is centered on the cross of Christ.

This was also Paul's experience with the Galatians, so he challenges them in Galatians 3:2: "I want to learn this from you. Did you receive the Spirit by the works of the law or by hearing of faith?"

Paul here cites the two fundamental methods of salvation. The phrase "works of the law" is a typical Pauline expression for legalism—that is, salvation by good works and law-observance. In Paul's day there was no equivalent Greek term for our English word "legalism", but the phrase "works of the law" means the same thing.

Paul is not against the law, but he opposes anyone who supports law-keeping as a means of salvation. In Galatians 5 Paul indeed upholds the law as a standard of Christian living—but not as a means of reaching heaven. Salvation comes only through Jesus Christ and Him crucified.

Saved by the Law?

Paul asks another question in Galatians 3:2: "Did you receive the Spirit by the observance of the law, using the law as a method of salvation, or did you receive the Spirit through faith in Jesus Christ as your Savior?"

The law requires each believer to personally obey it—without outside help. The individual must obey perfectly and continually if he or she wants to be saved through law-keeping (Galatians 3:10). Only under grace can God supply the Holy Spirit—who enables believers in real life to experience the righteous living they accept through faith in Jesus Christ.

The answer to Paul's question is obvious. The Galatians received the Holy Spirit by accepting Jesus Christ as their Savior. A legalist has no need or desire for a new-birth experience. The

Holy Spirit comes only to those who have accepted Jesus Christ as their Savior. Jesus reminded Nicodemus that he could not be saved by his own performance—he had to be born from above. In John 3:6 Jesus tells him in so many words: "That which is born of the flesh is flesh. Nicodemus, you need to be born from above; otherwise you can never enter the kingdom of heaven." The new birth comes only by faith in Jesus Christ.

Back to Legalism

In Galatians 3:3 Paul reminds his readers that they have "begun in the Spirit." Why are they now so foolish? How can they be so stupid? They began on a platform of justification by faith; by faith they have come under the umbrella of grace. But now they are turning back to legalism. Paul asks them, "Having begun in the Spirit, are you now being made perfect by the flesh?"

Paul is saying that the righteousness the Galatians received through faith in Jesus Christ is a perfect, complete righteousness. They can neither add to it nor improve upon it. Paul says in Galatians 5:4 that the moment Christians try to do this on their own, they fall from grace. It is either all of Christ's righteousness or none of it. Justification is by faith alone.

In verse 4 Paul reminds the Galatians of their past with yet another question: "Have you suffered so many things in vain—if indeed it was in vain?"

When the Galatians first accepted the gospel, they were persecuted; those who rejected the gospel opposed them. But they were willing to suffer because the joy of salvation was greater than all the suffering. Now Paul reminds them: "You suffered so greatly. You were willing to give up so much for this gospel. What has happened now? Why have you changed your mind?"

In verse 5 he finally concludes, "Therefore, He who supplies the Spirit to you and works miracles among you, does he do it by the works of the law or by the hearing of faith?"

The Jewish Christians, or Judaizers, have convinced the Galatians that salvation by faith is not enough—that they must factor in their own performance to the equation of salvation. They must be circumcised; they must do good works; and they must keep the law.

Paul is now saying, "Tell me, were you accepted as a child of God? Were you justified by faith alone or by faith *plus* other things that you added by your performance?"

The answer is obvious. The Galatians were justified by faith alone. They could add nothing to their salvation. Isaiah 64:6 says mankind's own righteousness is as filthy rags. Why? Because it is polluted with self. The only righteousness that qualifies the believer for heaven is the righteousness of Christ, and that righteousness is made effective by faith alone—not by faith *plus* something else.

Faith of Abraham

After reminding the Galatians of their experience in first accepting the gospel, Paul in Galatians 3:6 turns his attention to Abraham. Why Abraham?

Because to the Judaizers Abraham is both their most important ancestor and their example. Paul wants to remind these Gentiles that even the father of the Jews (and spiritual father of all who believe) was saved by faith alone. So Paul quotes Genesis 15:6 where Abraham's belief is "accounted to him for righteousness."

Paul adds in verse 7: "Therefore, know that only those who are of faith are sons of Abraham." He then quotes the Old Testament Scripture where God foretells that the entire human race will be blessed through Abraham: "And the Scripture, foreseeing that God would justify the Gentiles by faith, preached the gospel to Abraham beforehand, saying, 'In you all the nations shall be blessed.'"

Paul in Romans 4:13 speaks about Abraham as the father of all who believe: "For the promise that he would be the heir of the world was not to Abraham or to his seed through the law but through the righteousness of faith. For if those who are of the law are heirs, faith is made void and the promise made of no effect."

The moment believers add their own performance to their salvation, they deny that they are saved by grace alone.

Paul adds yet again, in Romans 4:15: "Because the law brings about wrath; for where there is no law there is no transgression."

The law does nothing to save sinners; rather it condemns them. The law does the very opposite of what the gospel does, for the law constantly demands perfect obedience of a person who looks to it for salvation. Paul adds in verse 16: "Therefore, it is of faith that it might be according to grace, so that the promise might be sure to all the seed."

He then defines what he means by "all the seed": "Not only to those who are of the law (*the Jews, who are the physical descendants of Abraham*) but also to those who are of the faith of Abraham who is the father of us all."

"Us all" here means all the believers—Jews and Gentiles alike. Paul brings this out in verse 17: "(As it is written, I have made you a father of many nations.)"

In what sense is Abraham father of all Christians? Verses 17 and 18 say: "In the presence of Him whom he believed, even God, who gives life to the dead and calls those things which do not exist as though they did; who, contrary to hope, in hope believed, so that he became the father of many nations, according to what was spoken, So shall your descendants be."

Abraham's Son Isaac

Paul makes this statement in context of the birth of Isaac, Abraham's son. In the biblical account, God promises the 75-year-old Abraham a son and Abraham believes God's promise and is accounted righteous. But God then waits almost 25 years to fulfill that promise—until Sarah is well past childbearing age.

Then God comes to Abraham again and asks, "Do you believe

I can give you a child?" Against hope—against all scientific evidence and human rationale—Abraham still takes God at His word.

Faith is not based on feelings, ability to perform, or scientific probability. Faith is based on the Word of God. Faith is taking God at His Word, and when God justifies a sinner through faith in Jesus Christ, the believer is convinced in his heart that he stands righteous in Christ even though he may not feel righteous.

Paul is saying that this is how Abraham was justified—Abraham, the prototype of all believers. Writing in Galatians 3:7, Paul says: "Therefore know only those who are of faith are Sons of Abraham." Christians today, like Abraham of old, are justified by faith alone in Jesus Christ.

Paul now continues in Galatians 3:8: "And the Scripture foreseeing that God would justify the nations (*Gentiles*) by faith, preached the gospel to Abraham beforehand, saying, 'In you all the nations shall be blessed.'"

God promised Abraham that one of his children would be the Messiah and in Galatians 4 Paul defines that seed (singular) as Christ. Through Him not only the Jews but the whole human race was saved. This salvation is *activated* by faith alone, as it was in Abraham.

In Galatians 3:27-29 we will discover that God uses one method, and one method alone, to save human beings. Whether in Old Testament times or New Testament times, whether male or a female, whether Jew or a Gentile, whether educated or uneducated, salvation always has and always will occur the same way. Becoming spiritual descendants of Abraham comes through faith alone.

Paul says in Galatians 3:26: "For you are all sons of God through faith in Christ Jesus." Isn't that beautiful? All believers become sons and daughters of God. Through Adam and Eve's rebellion all became children of the devil (Luke 4:5,6). But through grace, believers can regain their family status as sons and daughters of God the moment they believe in Jesus Christ as their Savior.

Paul adds in verse 27, "For as many of you as were baptized into Christ, have put on Christ, have become one with Christ through baptism."

This is why Jesus in Mark 16:15 and 16 commissions the disciples to "Go into all the world and preach this gospel to every creature. He who believes and is baptized, will be saved."

Paul is reminding the Christians that as many as are baptized into Christ have put on Christ. They have become one with Christ. His life becomes their life. His death becomes their death. His burial becomes their burial, and His resurrection becomes their resurrection (Romans 6:3-8).

Galatians 3:28 and 29 says, "There is neither Jew nor Greek, there is neither slave nor free, there is neither male nor female; for you are all one in Christ Jesus. And if you are Christ's, then you are Abraham's seed and heirs according to the promise."

The Jews mistakenly came to believe that God's people were limited to the physical descendants of Abraham, Isaac, and Jacob. But Paul makes it clear in Romans 9 and here in Galatians 3 that it is the faith of Abraham that makes a true Israelite.

Romans 9:6-8 teaches that a true Israelite is one who has the faith of Abraham; who has experienced the new birth from above as Isaac did; and whose faith endures to the end, like Jacob's when his name was changed to Israel—which means "One who Prevails."

Paul is telling the Galatians how absolutely foolish they are to turn from the pure gospel of grace alone to salvation by faith *plus* works. It's hopeless to try to marry these two methods of salvation. Either Christians select salvation by grace alone through faith in Jesus Christ or salvation by their own performance. It's one or the other. The two cannot mix.

Do Not Mix!

Why is it that human beings seem so prone to try to mix the two methods of salvation, and why is it that the moment "works" are added to "grace", grace gets cancelled out? Here are four explanations:

First, the gospel is good news only to those who have no confidence in themselves and rest entirely in Jesus Christ—this despite human nature's natural abhorrence of dependency (Philippians 3:3). Yet, the moment believers try to add their own works, they cease to depend fully on grace. This is the Galatian Christians' problem.

Second, many Christians fall into this trap of "I plus Christ" because they conclude that they must love God for Him to love them. The moment Christians begin performing good works to impress God, by definition they are rejecting His grace. God's *agape* love is unconditional; nothing a believer can do can add or detract from God's love for them (1 John 4:9 and 10).

Third, the flesh is proud, egocentric, and earnestly wants to make some contribution to salvation. Those who accept salvation by grace alone must admit that they are spiritual beggars. The moment they come to believe they possess their own spiritual capital, they push aside God's grace (Philippians 3:7-9).

And *finally*, mankind is by nature legalistic. Fallen humanity naturally wants to save itself through measurable performance. Once law-keeping becomes the currency of salvation, grace is pushed aside (Galatians 5:4).

Back in God's Grace

The book of Galatians is vital today because the problem of "partly by grace and partly by works" salvation is still alive and well among Christians today.

Yet, the two methods of salvation can never mix. May it

be our determined purpose to let nothing sidetrack us from the wonderful truth that salvation comes by grace alone, activated by faith in Jesus Christ.

Chapter 6

The True and False Gospel

Galatians 3:10-14

In Galatians 1 and 2 Paul strongly defends the divine origin of his apostolic calling and the gospel of grace he preaches, for both have come under fire from the Judaizers.

But in Galatians 3:1-9, covered last chapter, Paul goes on the offensive, pointing out to the Galatians how foolish they are in turning their backs on the gospel of grace alone and returning to a subtle form of legalism—salvation partly by grace and partly by performance.

Paul also reminds the Galatians that Abraham—not the Judaizers—is the true father of the Jews. Abraham is the true prototype of salvation for all men and he was justified by faith alone—nothing else.

We turn now to Galatians 3:10-14 as Paul contrasts the false gospel of the Judaizers with the true gospel. This is the fundamental theme Paul addresses throughout this epistle. The battle is between the true gospel that Paul proclaims and the false gospel the Judaizers are preaching.

Roads Never Meet

It will become absolutely apparent as we study this passage that the two gospel approaches depicted here produce opposite outcomes. Their destinations are mutually exclusive. They can never be harmonized and proclaimed as "two different pathways to the same destination."

With this in mind, let us read Galatians 3:10-14: "For as many as are of the works of the law are under the curse; for it is written, Cursed is everyone who does not continue in all things which are written in the book of the law, to do them. But that no one is justified by the law in the sight of God is evident, for the just shall live by faith. Yet the law is not of faith, but the man who does them shall live by them. Christ has redeemed us from the curse of the law, having become a curse for us; (for it is written, Cursed is everyone who hangs on a tree), that the blessing of Abraham might come upon the Gentiles in Christ Jesus, that we might receive the promise of the Spirit through faith."

Trusting in the Law

What does Paul mean when he writes, "For as many as are of the works of the law. . . ."? Clearly he is referring to all who rely on law-keeping as a means of salvation.

The word "rely" means depending on the law, or observance of the law, for salvation. Paul uses the phrase "the works of the law." We use the word "legalism" today. Such legalists, Paul says, are under a curse. Why? He quotes Deuteronomy 27:26 (the last book of the biblical law): "Cursed is everyone who does not confirm all words of this law."

In other words, those trying to be saved through the law must recognize two things: First, the law demands perfect obedience, and, second, this perfect obedience must be continual.

If a human being falls even once, he fails. It happened to Adam and Eve. God placed them in the Garden of Eden and gave them a commandment, and the very first time they sinned they came under the curse of the law. Those who wish to be saved by keeping the law must keep it perfectly and continually—an impossibility in this sinful world, as Paul writes in Galatians 3:11: "But that no one is justified by the law in the sight of God is evident."

None Righteous

What is the evidence to which Paul is referring? First, he speaks from the evidence of his own experience. If we are honest with ourselves, we recognize that all of us come up short in good works. Second, Paul says that humanity cannot match the biblical ideal. In Romans 3 he makes two telling references to human shortcomings compared with the biblical benchmark. The context is Romans 3:9, where he says: "What then? Are we better than they?" The "we" refers to the Jews and "they" refers to the Gentiles. Paul answers his own question: "Not at all. For we have previously charged (*or proved*) both Jews and Gentiles or Jews and Greeks, that they are all under sin (*"under" means "ruled by"*)."

He continues in Romans 3:10: "There is none righteous (*or none just*), no not even one." Scripture and experience both tell us that none is righteous—not even one. John concurs in 1 John 1:10 that anyone who says he has no sin is a liar.

Paul then re-emphasizes what he has written in Romans 3:10 by repeating it with only slight modification in verse 12: "There is none who does good, no, not one."

What Paul is saying in Galatians 3:11—that by the law none are justified—is absolutely evident, both from our subjective experiences and from the Word of God. Only one Man in this world has ever lived a perfect, sinless life—only the Lord, Jesus Christ, who did so that we might be saved.

Writing to the Galatians and citing clear evidence of Scripture, Paul now quotes Habbukuk 2:4 (his favorite, most oft-quoted text) in the last part of Galatians 3:11: "The just shall live by faith."

Scholars now agree that this text is better translated, "He that is just by faith shall live." This reading makes it clearer still that human beings can conquer the grave and obtain eternal life only through faith in Jesus Christ.

Paul continues in Galatians 3:12: "Yet the law is not of faith, but the man who does them shall live by them." What is Paul saying here? He's telling the Galatians that if they want to be saved by the law, it does no good to say to the law, "Law, we believe in every single commandment that you have given us."

The Jews believe the complete Torah (first five books of the Old Testament) and many Christians believe the Ten Commandments. But believing in these writings does not qualify a man or woman for salvation. Why? Because the law does not save through faith, it saves through performance. This makes the law method of salvation ineffective for a sinner. Paul says as much in Galatians 2:16: "By the works of the law shall no flesh be justified."

Peter's Lesson

Paul reminded the apostle Peter of this when he confronted him on the matter of refusing to eat with Gentiles in Antioch. The moment a person believes in Jesus Christ, he or she is no longer seen by God as a sinner. God imputes Christ's perfect righteousness to that person. But when a person decides to try to be saved by the law, his or her faith becomes meaningless, for the law cannot justify by faith. It justifies only when men and women practice perfect, persistent, continual obedience.

Curse of the Law

All have failed to keep the law perfectly. Paul reminds the believers in Romans 3:23 that there is no difference between Jew and Gentile, for all have sinned and come short of the glory of God. Paul says in Galatians 3:13 that Christ has redeemed mankind from the curse of the law, becoming a curse for us.

If we go back to Romans 3:19 where Paul concludes his discussion on the universal sin problem, he says that the whole world—Jews and Gentiles, everyone—stands condemned under the law of God. When God created mankind in Adam and placed him under the law, Adam came under the curse of a law the moment he sinned, and his descendants remain powerless to break it on their own. We are born on Death Row—hopelessly lost.

The incredible good news of the gospel, however, is that Christ has redeemed mankind from the curse of the law. When Paul quotes from Deuteronomy 21:23 and writes, "Cursed is everyone that hangs on a tree," he does so for an important reason. To understand it we need to look at the cross of Christ. In John 19 we discover, beginning in verse 5, after Christ's flogging that Pilate brings Jesus before the Jewish leaders, chief priests, scribes, and other onlookers and proclaims, "Behold the man." In other words, "Is this not enough?" But the Jews cry out, "Crucify Him! Crucify Him!"

The demand is strange, coming from Jews who never practice crucifixion themselves. The cross as a tool of execution was invented by Phoenicians about 600 years before Christ and was adopted by the Egyptians. The Romans took it from the Egyptians and refined it, using it to execute their runaway slaves and worst criminals. But the Jews never adopted crucifixion. Why then are they crying out to Pilate, "Crucify Him!" What do these Jews have in mind? There must be a reason, and we find it in John 19:7.

The Jews are crying out to Pilate—a representative of Rome who says he finds no fault in Jesus and no reason to condemn him. So the Jews tell him in so many words, "We have a law and according to our law he ought to die because he makes himself the Son of God."

Crucified for Blasphemy

The law the Jews are referring to is the law of blasphemy, found in Leviticus 24:16. It reads: "This is the law of blasphemy and whoever blasphemes the name of the Lord shall surely be put to death. And all the congregation shall certainly stone him. The stranger, as well as him who is born in the land, when he blasphemes the name of the Lord, he shall be put to death."

The law clearly demands death for blasphemy, but it also stipulates how the transgressor is to die—by *stoning*.

Do the Jews who reject Jesus as Messiah and Son of God and believe that His claim to be equal with the Father is blasphemy know that stoning is the required punishment? Certainly they do!

Now let us turn to John 10:30 where shortly before the crucifixion Jesus says that He and the Father are One. To the traditional Jew this is blasphemy. No wonder we read in John 10: 31, "The Jews took up stones again."

Clearly this is not the first time they have taken up stones to execute lawful judgment against a Man they believe to have blasphemed. But this still leaves the question, "Why do the Jews cry out to Pilate, 'Crucify Him?'"

Paul gives us the reason here, as he quotes Deuteronomy 21:23. "Cursed is everyone who hangs on a tree."

Most Jews of Jesus' day do not believe in an immortal soul. Unlike the Greeks who imported this idea into Palestine, most Jews believe that death is the end. If a Jew commits a sin worthy of death and the judge sentences him to death, he can fall on his knees before he is executed by stoning and ask God to forgive him. Forgiveness is available because of the daily morning and evening sacrifices in the Sanctuary.

But if the judge insists that the criminal be hung on a tree, this signifies to the Jews that the criminal must endure the irrevocable curse of God. It means good-bye to life forever. It means that the transgressor has committed an unpardonable sin.

When the Jews cry "Crucify Him!" they have this text in mind, for they view crucifixion the same as being hanged on a tree. The reason the Jews cry "Crucify Him" is because on more than one occasion Christ predicted His resurrection on the third day (John 2:16-22). To make sure Christ would not rise from the dead, they cried "Crucify Him" so that God would curse Him.

This is why when the disciples preach the gospel to the Jews in the early days of the Christian church, often they substitute the word "tree" for "cross."

For example, Acts 5:30, Acts 10:39, Acts 13:29, and 1 Peter 2:24 all use the word "tree" in the original text. Each statement in these passages is directed to Jews. Why? Because crucifixion is identified with hanging on a tree. So when the Jews cry out, "Crucify Him!" they are demanding not only death but that God should curse this Man for being a blasphemer. This is why the resurrection of Christ is the greatest proof God gives the Jewish nation that Christ is the Messiah.

John 7:30 and John 8:20 both declare that when the Jews try to kill Jesus by stoning, they fail because His hour has not yet come. We read in Luke 22:53 Jesus' words to the angry mob when He is taken captive in Gethsemane: "This is your hour and the prince of darkness. . ."

At Gethsemane God removes His protection so the Jews can crucify Jesus. To the Jews the cross means the curse of God. Isaiah 53:4 prophesies of Jesus, "We did esteem Him stricken and smitten of God. . ."

But does God allow Jesus to be cursed for blasphemy? No. God allows Jesus to be crucified, as Romans 8:31 and 32 explains, because He "spared not His own Son but delivered Him up for us all."

At the cross God allows the curse of *all* sin that belongs to humanity to fall upon Jesus Christ. Jesus does not die for His own sin, for He has no sin of His own. When Jesus dies on the cross, he suffers more than physical torture. One writer suggests that Jesus hardly feels the physical torture, for He is suffering the far greater effects of the irrevocable curse of God. This—not the physical torture of the cross is what makes the death of Christ a supreme sacrifice.

Tasting Our Death

Jesus tastes death for every human being (Hebrews 2:9). By His own death he abolishes death and brings immortality and life through the gospel (2 Timothy 1:10). That which makes the cross of Christ the supreme sacrifice is not the torture of crucifixion but the curse of God on Jesus Christ as our Sin-bearer.

As Jesus hangs on the cross, He cannot see through the portals of the tomb. He sees no hope of resurrection. He feels that sin is so offensive that His separation from God must be eternal and He cries out in agony, "My God, My God, why hast Thou forsaken Me?" God, who is Light (1 John 1:5) withdraws His presence from Christ and as a result the land is enshrouded in darkness (Matthew 27:45). This is what leads Christ to cry out "Father, Father, why have you forsaken Me?" (Matthew 27:46).

Jesus had cried out in Gethsemane, sweating blood, "Father, if it is possible, remove the cup." The cup is not the cross, but the irrevocable curse of God—the wrath of God poured upon Him without mercy. This is Jesus' supreme sacrifice. This is the sacrifice that redeems humanity from the curse of the law. Jesus becomes a curse for humanity. His Father has not turned against Jesus, but because the Father so loves the world He gives up His only begotten Son.

Hope of Resurrection

Jesus hangs on the cross, abandoned by the Father, yet totally dependent on His Father for resurrection. He has said more than once, "I can do nothing of Myself (John 5:19, 30)."

Now on the cross the Father has apparently forsaken Him—He abandons Jesus who now treads the winepress alone (Isaiah 63:3). The devil comes to Jesus three times, according to Luke 23:35-39. Satan comes tempting Jesus, through the soldiers, once through the priests, and once through the thief on the left-hand side.

The temptations are fierce: "Come down and save Yourself. Stop being a Fool. These people are mocking You. They have crucified You. Why are You laying down Your life for them?"

But on the cross Jesus reveals a most significant truth. Though He can physically come down and save Himself, He cannot save

Himself and the world at the same time. He has to make a choice and He chooses to "die that they might live." Paul tells us in Romans 5:8 that God demonstrates His self-emptying—*agape*—love in that Jesus died for humanity.

On the cross Jesus demonstrates that He loves humanity more than He loves Himself. This is the God we worship. This is Jesus Christ, the Savior of all mankind. He redeems us from the curse of the law at infinite cost to Himself. Paul writes in Romans 10:4 that Christ is the end—the completion of the law for righteousness to everyone who believes.

Self-help Redemption?

So we return to Galatians. Truly anyone who rejects this gospel and tries to achieve salvation through performance deserves to be called foolish.

Paul says in Galatians 3:14 "that the blessing of Abraham might come upon the Gentiles (*upon us*) in Christ Jesus, that we might receive the promise of the Spirit through faith."

No human being—no philosopher, however convincing—can present a more compelling picture of salvation than the one found in the New Testament. The New Testament is clear. Humanity is saved by grace alone. Believers are saved by the doing and dying of Jesus Christ—and nothing else. Salvation is guaranteed, as long as faith in Jesus Christ Savior remains unmovable. But the day a believer turns his or her back on this truth, Paul says in Galatians 5:4, "You have fallen from grace and Christ is made of no effect to you."

May all who are reading these lines hold fast to their faith, justified by faith now and to the end.

Chapter 7
Law vs. Promise

Galatians 3:15-29

Paul has now proved from Old Testament Scripture (Galatians 3:10-14) that God saves sinners through faith in Christ alone and that law keeping and good works contribute nothing to salvation.

In this chapter we look at a passage in which Paul uses Jewish logic to prove that Christians are saved by God's promise—not by the law. The argument is summed up in Galatians 3:15-29, but we will analyze it in three stages, beginning with verses 15-18. These four verses deal with the changeless promise of God.

We will then move to verses 19-25, where Paul explains the purpose of the law, and finally to verses 26-29, where Paul discusses the meaning of being heirs of the kingdom of God.

God's Will and Testament

Galatians 3:15-18 has important lessons for us, despite its deeply Jewish logic: "Brethren, I speak in the manner of men: Though it is only a man's covenant, yet if, it is confirmed, no one annuls or adds to it. Now to Abraham and his Seed were the promises made. He does not say, 'And to seeds,' as of many, but as of one, 'And to your Seed' who is Christ. And this I say, that the law which was 430 years later, cannot annul the covenant that was confirmed before God in Christ, that it should make the promise of no effect. For if the inheritance is of the law, it is no longer of promise; but God gave it to Abraham by promise."

What is Paul trying to prove here? First, he uses a legal will of his day to illustrate God's promise to mankind. In verse 15 he says, "Brethren, I speak in the manner of men: though it is only a man's covenant, yet, if it is confirmed, no one annuls or adds to it."

The Greek custom in Paul's day is that once a will is made, signed, and sealed, it cannot be changed. Using this model, he now tells the Galatians in verse 16 that God has made a will, or promise, to Abraham that "in thy seed shall all the nations be blessed."

The word "seed" in the promise is in the singular. Though it may seem strange to the Western way of thinking, in Jewish thought the word "seed" has a corporate significance, similar to the word "Adam." As the word "Adam" includes the whole human race in the Jewish mind, so Paul is telling the Galatians that the word "seed" here affects the whole human race through one Person.

This one Person is Jesus Christ, as Paul makes clear in the last part of verse 16, "And to your seed who is Christ."

God created all mankind in one man—Adam—and when Adam sinned, condemnation came upon all. Likewise when Christ obeyed, justification of life came unto all men (Romans 5:12-21), for Jesus, the Seed of Abraham, is the second Adam—the second mankind. Jesus is not just one man among many men but the whole human race, gathered together in Him. This is why Paul in Corinthians calls Him the last Adam (1 Corinthians 15:45).

A Permanent Promise

Paul tells the Galatians in verse 17 that the promise God made to Abraham is that in this Seed (Christ) the whole world will be blessed irrevocably—this promise cannot be changed or done away with through the law, which comes on the scene 430 years after God makes the promise to Abraham.

Paul is saying that the law given through Moses does not change in any way God's earlier promise to Abraham. Salvation through the law and salvation through grace, we have already discovered, are two opposite systems of salvation that simply do not mix.

The law says, "Thou shalt" and "Thou shall not. . . ." But the promise of God is still, "I shall save you in spite of the fact that you are a sinner." The law saves based on perfect performance of good deeds. But the promise of God saves the ungodly through faith in God's work in Christ (Romans 4:5).

All non-Christian religions are based on salvation by performance. But God's way of saving mankind is through grace—a gift offered to mankind. Paul is saying that God in delivering the law to the Jewish nation could not, and did not, annul or change the promise he made 430 years before to Abraham. The promise made to Abraham is unchangeable.

Paul tells the Galatians in verse 18, "For if the inheritance is of the law, it is no longer a promise; But God gave it to Abraham by promise."

The moment we try to add the law as a requirement for salvation, salvation ceases to be a promise. God gave Abraham the promise of salvation as a gift (or will) some 430 years before the codified law appeared on the scene.

But if mankind is saved entirely by the promise of God to Abraham, why does God give the law 430 years later? Is God saying to Moses, "By the way, when I gave the promise of salvation to Abraham, I totally forgot a very important item—the law! So I am giving the law to you, Moses—better late than never—to make up for what I failed to give to Abraham!"

No! God never tells Moses that the law is being added as an extra requirement for salvation.

Why Then the Law?

But this still leaves the question, "Why then does God give the law through Moses 430 years after He promises by a will that He will save all men through Abraham's Seed, Jesus Christ?

Paul supplies both question and answer in Galatians 3:19-25. The passage reads: "What purpose then does the law serve? It was added because of transgressions, till the seed should come to whom the promise was made; and it was appointed through angels by the hand of a mediator. Now a mediator does not mediate for one only, but God is one. Is the law then against the promises of God? Certainly not! For if there had been a law given which would have given life, truly righteousness would have been by the law. But the Scripture has confined all under sin, that the promise by faith in Jesus Christ might be given to those who believe. But before faith came, we were kept under guard by the law, kept for the faith which would after be revealed. Therefore, the law was our tutor to bring us to Christ, that we might be justified by faith. But after faith has come, we are no longer under a tutor."

Paul first asks a question in this rather complicated passage: "What purpose then, does the law serve?" Why does God add the law 430 years after He promises salvation to Abraham as a gift? The answer comes quickly—"Because of transgression."

Three Words for "Sin"

There are 12 different words for "sin" used by Old Testament writers, but all 12 are based on only three root words. The first root word for "sin" simply means missing the mark, coming short of the glory of God. Paul brings this out in Romans 3:23.

The second word for sin is often translated "iniquity" in the Bible and literally means to be crooked or bent. When Isaiah tells us in Isaiah 53:6 that all we like sheep have gone astray and turned to our own way, he is speaking of a condition. David in Psalm 51:5 says that he was shaped in iniquity from his mother's womb. Iniquity is humanity's selfish bent its sinful nature.

The third word for sin is often translated "transgression", which means a deliberate violation of a law. The prerequisite for transgression is knowledge of the law. From Adam to Moses the human race continually sins, as Paul brings out in Romans 5:13. But the moment God gives the law through Moses, that sinning moves into the category of transgressing—willful, deliberate violation of known law.

The law does nothing to solve the sin problem—in fact it

accentuates the problem, for it serves as a continual reminder that humanity deserves death. In verse 20, Paul says, "Now, a mediator does not mediate for only one but God is one."

This text is difficult to understand on first reading. In the Greek, two separate words can each be translated as "covenant" in English. One Greek word refers to a *will*, the other to a *contract*.

One person makes a *will* that may affect many, but a *contract* is made between two persons or parties. The giving of the law is like a contract. God gives the law and the Jews say, "All that you have said we will do."

But the real reason God gives the law, says Paul in Galatians 3: 21 and onward, is to convince humanity of its sinfulness and need of a Savior. The law is not intended to assist in salvation, except as it persuades sinful human beings of their need for a Savior.

Galatians 3:21 and 22 says, "Is the law then against the promise of God?" Did God change His mind and take back his promise of salvation and instead offer a contract? Did God change the will He made to Abraham? Certainly not! If God had intended man to be saved by keeping laws, there would have been no need of a promise. God gave the law to convince mankind of its sinfulness and need of a Savior. The law was designed to help make the good news of the gospel even more desirable.

The Deceit of Sin

Sin is transgression of the law, but sin also deceives. Sin tells the sinner that he or she is not a bad person—that through willpower it is possible to live a life worthy of salvation (read Jeremiah 17:9).

Sin tempts us to look God in the eye and say, "God, You give us the rules. We'll keep them and You give us life."

But when we realize that the law demands perfection of thought, perfection of obedience, perfection of nature, it dawns on us that by doing the works of the law we can never become just before God.

God gave the law to convince the human race that it is a prisoner to sin and desperately in need of a Savior.

Before Faith Came?

Now we come to verse 23: "But before faith came. . ." There is a word missing in this statement that can be disconcerting. The word "faith" in the original is preceded by the definite article "the." Paul is actually saying, "Before the faith came."

Without the definite article the word "faith" could mean the believer's faith, but Paul is not discussing the believer's faith. He is saying, "Before the faith," or "Before the Source of our faith which is Jesus Christ."

Verse 23 says that before Christ, the Seed, came, humanity was kept under guard by the law—kept for the faith that would afterward be revealed.

When God gave the law through Moses, the sinful human race suddenly became guilty of transgression. Before the law was given, mankind was not accountable for its transgressions. Paul brings this out clearly in Romans 5:13 when he says that where there is no law, God has no right to legally accuse mankind of sin, but the moment God gives the law, the human race has no more excuse for sinning.

Paul is saying that the law condemns the whole human race, imprisoning it on Death Row until Christ comes to set it free.

Historically speaking the whole human race is under condemnation, legally and lawfully, from Moses until Christ. Paul explains in verse 24 that the law is a tutor. A better translation for tutor is "guardian." The Greek word Paul uses has a special meaning not readily understood today—that of a trusted slave used by the master to discipline and look after his child.

Because there were no public schools in those days, education was often supplied by private tutors. A trusted slave would hold the young child's hand and take him to the home of the tutor.

This child had no way of escaping until the slave delivered him to the tutor's house. Then and only then was he released.

Paul says here that the law acts like a guardian—like a policeman who holds us securely in his grip until Christ comes on the scene to justify us by faith in the promise of God.

The Law Prepares the Way

From Adam to Christ salvation was based on a promise. Abraham was saved by a promise. So was Noah. To make the promise even more meaningful, however, God gave the law through Moses. The law did not, and does not, save—it simply offers convincing proof that all are sinners in need of a Savior.

The arrival of the law actually made humanity's situation appear far worse than before. God's purpose in giving the law was to make the promise of salvation in Jesus Christ even more desirable and meaningful.

For example, if I offer a plate of fine food to someone who has just come from a banquet, the food will have little appeal. But if that same person has eaten no food for three days, he will accept my gift with deep gratitude. The same applies here. God gave the law to show humanity how sinful it truly is—that it is sinful by nature 100 percent of the time.

Paul says in Galatians 2:16 that by the works of the law no human being will ever make it to heaven. The law simply puts humanity on Death Row, with no hope of escape until Christ opens the door.

When Christ came and perfectly satisfied the demands of the law by His life and death, He redeemed all mankind. That is the promise of God; this is salvation by grace. This salvation is made effective by faith alone—nothing more, nothing less (Romans 10:4).

Free from the Law

Paul concludes this section in Galatians 3:25: "But after the faith has come. . . ."

After Christ came historically, the human race is no longer under the law because now there is another umbrella—another platform by which man is saved, known as grace. No, humanity is not born under grace automatically. Paul is dealing here with the objective facts of the gospel, and the facts are that God so loved the world that He gave us His only begotten Son. This is God's gift to mankind. But like any other gift, it cannot be enjoyed until we accept it. The way we accept the gift of God is not by *doing* something but by *believing*—by faith in Jesus Christ. The moment we believe in Jesus Christ, we pass from condemnation to justification, from death to life (John 5:24).

Identifying with Christ

Paul is writing to baptized Christian believers who have been sidetracked from the pure gospel through the teachings of Judaizers. After proving that salvation comes by grace alone and explaining the purpose of the law, Paul reassures his readers in Galatians 3: 26-29: "For you are all sons of God through faith in Christ Jesus. For as many of you as were baptized into Christ have put on Christ. There is neither Jew nor Greek, there is neither slave nor free, there is neither male nor female; for you are all one in Christ Jesus. And if you are Christ's, then you are Abraham's seed, and heirs according to the promise." What a wonderful statement!

The New Testament refers to Jesus as the Son of God. By joining Himself to the corporate human race and rewriting humanity's history, Jesus gives us the privilege of becoming sons and daughters of God by uniting us with Him through faith. Paul is saying in verse 26 that all believers, by their faith union in Christ and by abiding in Christ, become sons and daughters of God.

John writes, "Behold, what manner of love the Father has bestowed on us that we should be called children of God" (1 John 3:1). Faith is not simply a mental assent to truth. Faith means identifying with Jesus Christ and Him crucified. At the incarnation, God put all men into Christ so that He became the second Adam. By faith all are free to identify themselves with Christ and His holy history. This happens at baptism. Galatians 3:27 says, "For as many of you as were baptized into Christ. . . . "

Notice that baptism is always into Christ. Paul brings this out clearly in Romans 6:3-5 where he says that baptism into Christ means specifically baptism into Christ's death. His death becomes the new Christian's death. His burial becomes the new Christian's burial. His resurrection becomes the new Christian's resurrection.

In the early Christian church baptism was always by immersion, offering a beautifully complete identification with Jesus Christ who was crucified, buried, and resurrected.

Paul now says in verse 28 that the moment a person is baptized, all distinctions of race, gender, and class privilege disappear. In the Christian church there is no qualitative distinction between Jew and Gentile, between slave and master, or between male or female, for all are one in Christ.

The Head is Jesus Christ; the church is the body. The believer becomes one with Christ and joins the Seed of Abraham through whom God promises salvation.

Paul now concludes in verse 28: "And if you are Christ's, then you are Abraham's seed and heirs according to the promise." May this be our experience. May this be the platform on which we stand.

Chapter 8
From Slaves to Sons and Daughters

Galatians 4:1-11

God's promise to Abraham that through his Seed (singular) salvation would come to all mankind was neither annulled nor superceded at Sinai, and this study continues that theme of thought.

Last chapter we learned that 430 years after making this promise to Abraham, God proclaimed His law to the human race through Moses. But this law had existed from the beginning in the hearts of men—in their consciences.

Paul brings this out clearly in Romans 2:14-16. But when God hands the law in explicit, written form to Moses, sin no longer is defined as only missing the mark. It now becomes transgression—a legal offense.

This means that from Moses until Christ mankind stood condemned, both for Adam's sin and their personal sins. The giving of the law made the human race legally accountable for its actions (See Romans 3:19 and 20).

Reared by a Slave

Paul compares the human experience in the 1,500 years between Moses and Christ as that of a nobleman's child entrusted to a worthy slave.

By Roman tradition a child of a wealthy man who is one day to inherit his father's estate is placed at a very young age under the discipline of a trusted slave. The youngster remains with this slave until the boy reaches an age of sufficiency, sometime between the boy's 14th and 17th years. The father sets the date, known as the son's day of *Liberlia*.

On that date the son receives his own special gown, or toga, and amid tremendous festivity is released from the discipline of the trusted slave. From that day forward the young man is free.

Paul compares this child to the human race in the years between Moses and Christ. In Galatians 4, especially the first seven verses, he says that human beings are no different than the child under the discipline of a slave.

Slavery to Son-ship

Galatians 4:1-7 picks up the thought where Chapter 3 leaves off. Speaking of how believers move from slavery to son-ship, Paul writes: "Now I say that the heir, as long as he is a child, does not differ at all from a slave, though he is master of all, but is under guardians and stewards until the time appointed by the father. Even so we, when we were children, were in bondage under the elements of the world. But when the fullness of the time had come, God sent forth His Son, born of a woman, born under the law, to redeem those who were under the law that we might receive the adoption of sons. And because you are sons, God has sent forth the Spirit of His Son into your hearts, crying out, Abba, Father! Therefore you are no longer a slave but a son, and if a son, then an heir of God through Christ."

What a wonderful passage.

Let's study it step by step.

The first two verses describe the Roman coming-of-age process we've already cited. Paul is saying: "Now I say that the heir, as long as he is a child, does not differ at all from a slave though he is master of all." The child of a rich man will one day inherit all that belongs to his father. In actual fact this child is wealthy, but as long as he is a child he remains under the discipline of the trusted slave. This means the son has no more freedom than the slave himself. He is not his own master; he must do whatever the slave tells him to do.

From the time he is handed over to the slave until his father sets him free, he is no different than the slave. Only the father knows when he will be set free, and he may tell his son, "On your 14^{h} (or 15th, 16th, or 17^{h}) birthday you shall be liberated from the authority of that slave."

When the date finally arrives, a great party is given in the boy's honor, and he puts on his new toga, which symbolizes his newfound freedom from the slave.

Using this illustration from Roman society, Paul writes in Galatians 4:4: "But when the fullness of the time had come (*the appointed time that God promised Abraham*), God sent forth His Son, born of a woman, born under the law." Paul is telling us that in the incarnation God did something very special. He took the divine life of His Son and the corporate life of the human race and united these two in the womb of Mary. That is why He is called Emmanuel, God with us. This union did not save humanity; it had no redemptive value, except that it qualified Jesus to legally become our Substitute.

The Christian Dilemma

One of the most difficult problems in presenting the gospel to the non-Christian world (*approximately 70 percent of world's population at this time*) is the ethical issue of the gospel, a problem that existed throughout the Christian era and especially since the Reformation: "How can one Man be the Savior of all men?"

How can an innocent Man, Jesus Christ, bear the guilt and punishment of the guilty human race? No law, God's or man's, allows guilt and punishment to be transferred from the guilty to the innocent. God makes this clear in Deuteronomy 24:16 and repeats it in Ezekiel 18:1-20. Guilt cannot be transferred. Righteousness cannot be transferred from one person to another. No law allows this.

How, then, can God justify the ungodly through Jesus Christ

and still maintain the integrity of His holy law? This became a central issue during the Reformation as Roman Catholic scholars accused the Reformers of creating "legal fiction." Today the same accusation of "legal fiction" is voiced by Muslim scholars.

We find the answer in the fact that before God could save humanity in Christ, He had to legally qualify Christ to become its Savior. He did this by uniting the divine life of Christ with the corporate human life that needed redeeming. Divinity was united to corporate humanity in Mary's womb. Jesus became the second Adam under the law as mankind's Substitute and Representative.

This truth is beautifully explained in 1 Corinthians 1:30: "But of Him, you are in Christ Jesus. . ." Notice, three people are involved in that statement. "Him" refers to God the Father; the "You", in plural form, refers to humanity; and Christ is the second Person of the Godhead, the Son of God.

Paul is saying that God took the corporate human race—corporate human life—and joined it to Christ in Mary's womb. In so doing Christ and humanity became one and Jesus was legally qualified to become the second *Adam* ("Adam" in Hebrew means "Mankind"—See Genesis 5:2 where "Adam" is translated "Mankind").

Paul says in 1 Corinthians 1:30: "But of Him you are in Christ Jesus who became for us wisdom from God." The word "*wisdom*" in the Greek means special knowledge. Jesus says in John 8:32: "You shall know the truth and the truth shall set you free." What is this truth? By uniting humanity to Christ and by His perfect life and sacrificial death, Christ became humanity's righteousness, its sanctification, and its redemption. Paul says in verse 31 that as it is written, he who glories let him glory in the Lord.

Children of God

Returning now to Galatians 4:4 and 5, Paul tells us that when the right time came—when the appointed time arrived—God sent forth His Son, born of a woman, born under law. Christ united

Himself with us and became what we are. In doing so He became qualified to save the human race and by His dying to redeem mankind from under the law and adopt it as sons and daughters into His family. Paul is saying that in Jesus Christ, God gave mankind a new history in which to stand perfect before God's law. This new status—this clean slate—is God's gift. The moment human beings accept that gift by faith, they become children of God. In Galatians 4:6 Paul says, "And because you are sons, God has sent forth the Spirit of His Son into our hearts, crying out, Abba, Father!"

Romans 8:16 and 17 says the same thing even more clearly: "The Spirit Himself bears witness with our spirit that we are children of God, and if children, then heirs—heirs of God and joint heirs with Christ, if indeed we suffer with Him, that we may also be glorified together."

On the cross the corporate life of the human race, which stands condemned to death, died in Christ. Not for three days but forever, thus meeting the just demands of the law. In exchange God so loved the world that He gave mankind the eternal life of His Son in the resurrection (the meaning of John 3:16). This is God's supreme gift to the human race (1 John 5:11, 12).

Christians not only receive forgiveness and justification, they become sons and daughters of God. They are no longer members of this world. They become citizens of heaven, joint heirs with Christ.

Paul clearly says in Romans 5:15-21 that what humanity receives in Christ is much more than what it lost in Adam.

Both the Old Testament and the New Testament book of Hebrews explain that Adam was created a little lower than the angels. God stands above all, next come angels, and then come human beings, created a little lower than the angels (Psalm 8:4,5; Hebrews 2:6-8).

Adam sinned and brought the human race to the bottom of the pit—onto Death Row with no way of escape except through Jesus Christ.

But Christ joined Himself to the human race and became a second Adam, not only releasing mankind from its death sentence but elevating it *above* the angels. He adopts those who accept his gift as heirs authorized to rule and judge angels. What over-abundant grace! In Christ mankind is far more exalted than it was in Adam, even before sin (Revelation 20:6; 22:5).

No Moaning, No Groaning

Some moan and groan: "Why did God allow sin to enter this world?" Theologians answer this important question in various ways, but often forgotten is the fact that through adoption into the family of Jesus, victorious mankind rises far higher than it could in Adam. Those who accept Christ receive the Holy Spirit in their hearts—the new birth experience, which makes them sons and daughters of God and co-heirs with Christ. Through the new birth experience believers become God's children who can address Him as "Dear Father."

Paul is saying to us in verse 7, "You are no longer a slave but a son. If you are a son, then you are an heir of God through Christ. What a privilege this is!"

Having clearly explained the situation, in verses 8-11 Paul speaks about his great fear for the Galatian Christians: "But then, indeed, when you did not know God, you served those which by nature are not gods. But now after you have known God, or rather are known by God, how is it that you turn again to the weak and beggarly elements, to which you desire again to be in bondage? You observe days and months and seasons and years. I am afraid for you, lest I have labored for you in vain."

Beggarly Elements

When the Galatians were still pagans, worshipping false gods, they had no joy. They had no peace and no hope, either, because in all pagan religions salvation comes through performance.

Since human beings who strive on their own always come up short of the mark, legalists and those who worship false gods experience little peace or joy. They end up serving beggarly elements—the "dos" and "don'ts" found in all performance-based religions. They are in bondage. They observe days and months and seasons, hoping to appease the angry gods.

The Galatians joyfully gave up their pagan ways when they heard Paul preach the gospel. With heartfelt gratitude they accepted Jesus Christ as their Savior, so much so that they told Paul they were willing to pluck out their own eyes and donate them to Paul because of the problem he was facing with his eyesight.

But now the Judaizers have convinced the Galatians that they must return to bondage—that they must again look to the "dos" and "don'ts" as requirements for salvation. The Galatians are trapped in a subtle form of legalism, and with a pastor's heart, Paul pleads with them, "Have I labored with you in vain?" In other words, "Have I given you the good news for nothing, now that you have turned your backs on the gospel?"

Paul is deeply concerned for the Galatian Christians, for though Paul is a theologian, he has the heart of a pastor—a heart that longs to see the Galatians saved in Christ.

"How can you do it?" Paul cries. "How can you turn from the good news of salvation to joyless, hopeless legalism?"

Paul's Plea Today

The devil is very much alive today, and just as he sidetracked the Galatian Christians through the Judaizers, Satan would like to do the same in the church today. Christians must come to grips with Paul's Epistle to the Galatians, for it has been recorded for their benefit upon whom the ends of the world would come.

Man by nature is legalistic. One young Christian who decided to adopted legalism once told me why: "I must work for anything I need in this world. Why should salvation be different?"

But God's ways are not man's ways. The prophet Isaiah tells us that as far as the stars are—many, many light years away—so are God's ways compared to ours (Isaiah 55:8,9).

In this world we do work for everything we gain, for this world and its ways are molded by the curse of sin. God told Adam after his rebellion, "By the sweat of the brow, you will eat your bread" (Genesis 3:19).

But no amount of human sweat can save us, for we are slaves to sin. Paul makes it abundantly clear in Galatians 2:16, "By the works of the law, shall no flesh be justified."

God's way of saving sinners is through faith in Jesus Christ. Salvation is by grace alone. This is the wonderful truth Luther and his fellow Reformers restored after the Dark Ages.

The Devil at Work

Grace alone through faith alone—these are the two wonderful truths of the gospel restored to the church by the Reformers. But the devil, through modern liberal theology, is still trying to sidetrack the church from the pure gospel of Jesus Christ.

Yes, we live in a scientific age. Mankind has made tremendous advances in technology, but the scientific method cannot redeem sinful humanity. We need a Savior, and the good news is that God sent a Messiah by whom all can be redeemed.

I plead with those who have not yet accepted Jesus as Savior to do so now. There is no other name under heaven by which we can be saved. And to those already rejoicing in Christ I say, never allow any human being to rob you of your wonderful peace and joy in Jesus Christ.

Law vs. Grace

Let us consider, in closing, the distinctive markers that set apart law- vs. grace-driven religion.

First, religion under law is a religion of fear, for those who practice it are constantly living under the law's curse. Those living under grace, however, experience love, joy, and peace.

1 John 4:17,18 says that perfect love—the love of God—casts out fear. As Christ is, so are we, for we stand perfect in Christ through faith.

Second, religion of law is a religion of insecurity. Mankind today faces massive insecurity. But under grace there is full assurance of salvation, for the Christian knows in whom he or she believes and that God is able to save to the uttermost all who come to God through Jesus Christ (Hebrews 7:25).

Finally, religion under law ends in spiritual poverty, bankruptcy, and burnout. A time comes when the law-driven Christian gives up because his or her performance never reaches the requirement of the law. But those under the umbrella of grace never tire of following the Lord, for they have peace with God.

May all who read this book cling to the message of salvation by grace alone. May nobody steal your peace, joy, and assurance of salvation in Christ.

Chapter 9
The Effects of Legalism
Galatians 4:12-20

In the first three chapters of Galatians Paul presents himself as an apostle of Jesus Christ, a theologian, and defender of the faith. Now in Galatians 4:12-20 we meet Paul, the passionate lover of the flock.

He appeals with great tenderness to the Galatians, referring to them as his brethren. Paul is a Jew; the Galatians are Gentiles. For Paul to call these Gentiles "brothers" shows tremendous Christian development, pastoral tenderness and acceptance.

He calls them "my dear children" or "little children," echoing the words of the apostle John, the disciple of love. But in Galatians 4:19 Paul goes even further than John, likening himself to a mother who is in labor until Christ is formed in his children, the Galatians.

Not only does the Judaizers' legalism endanger their salvation, says Paul, but it has split a once-loving church into factions. He writes in Galatians 5:15: "But if you bite and devour one another, beware lest you be consumed by one another."

The doctrine of justification by faith tells us that we are all 100 percent sinners, saved by grace. But the moment we determine to be saved by being good (legalism), we begin to compare ourselves with one another. Just as the Pharisees did in the days of Christ, legalists always begin to judge one another on the basis of performance.

The Results of Legalism

Paul writes in Galatians 4:12-20: "Brethren, I urge you to become as I am, for I am as you are. You have not injured me at all.

You know that because of physical infirmity I preached the gospel to you at the first. And my trial which was in my flesh you did not despise or reject, but you received me as an angel of God, even as Christ Jesus. What then was the blessing you enjoyed? For I bear you witness that, if possible, you would have plucked out your own eyes and given them to me. Have I therefore become your enemy because I tell you the truth? They zealously court you but for no good; yes, they want to exclude you, that you may be zealous for them. But it is good to be zealous in a good thing always, and not only when I am present with you. My little children, for whom I labor in birth again until Christ is formed in you, I would like to be present with you now and to change my tone for I have doubts about you."

Paul is writing as a deeply concerned pastor to his flock in Galatia. He knows what legalism does to a church and writes in verse 12: "Brethren, I urge you to become as I am, for I am as you are."

There was a time, Paul is saying, when he was like these Judaizers—a believer in legalism. But he has given it all up for the gospel. In verse 12 Paul urges the Galatians, "Please, follow my example."

He expresses the same idea in Philippians 3:3: "For we are the circumcision who worship God in the Spirit, rejoice in Christ Jesus and have no confidence in the flesh."

To Paul a genuine Christian is one who depends totally on Christ for salvation, and recognizes that as complete sinners they are saved only by grace.

In Philippians 3:4 he continues, "Though I also might have confidence in the flesh, if anyone else thinks he may have confidence in the flesh, I more so."

The word "flesh" here refers to anything that belongs to the Christian by human nature. This includes family status, ability, standing in the church—anything a Christian may be tempted to depend upon for full or partial salvation. He is telling the Philippians that if anyone can brag about what he has accomplished through his own effort, Paul can.

In verses 5 and 6 Paul explains why. Paul was as a Pharisee, a man zealous for God and zealous for the law. He writes in Philippians 3:5,6: "Circumcised the eighth day of the stock of Israel, of the tribe of Benjamin, a Hebrew of the Hebrews, concerning the law, a Pharisee, concerning zeal (*zeal for God*), persecuting the church, concerning the righteousness which is in the law, blameless." Paul had seen himself before conversion as a very successful believer in God.

After his conversion, he writes in verses 7-9, "But, what things were gain to me, these I have counted loss for Christ. But indeed I also count all things loss for the excellence of the knowledge of Christ Jesus my Lord, for whom I have suffered the loss of all things, and count them as rubbish that I may gain Christ. And be found in him (*Christ*), not having my own righteousness, which is from the law, but that which is through faith in Christ, the righteousness which is from God by faith."

Paul knows what it means to be a legalist! But when he finds Jesus Christ and His righteousness, legalism no longer has any meaning for him. It becomes as filthy rags—rubbish.

Pleading with the Galatians

Paul is begging the Galatian Christians in so many words, "Please don't turn back to legalism. Please become like me, as I became like you. I too accepted Jesus Christ as you did at the beginning."

In Galatians 4:13 and 14 he says, "You know that, because of physical infirmities, I preached the gospel to you at the first. And my trial, which was in my flesh, you did not despise or reject but you received me as an angel of God even as Christ Jesus."

An Emotional Appeal

Paul is appealing to their emotions and past experience, reminding them that when he first came to Galatia and preached the gospel, he was suffering terrible problems with his eyes. Some scholars suggest that this condition was a carry-over from Paul's Damascus experience, but all we really know is that his eyes must have looked awful. Yet the Galatians didn't let this bother them. They were willing to ignore Paul's unsightly condition because they so appreciated the gospel he was bringing them.

In verse 15 Paul says that they valued his message so much that they were willing to pluck out their own eyes and give them to him in gratitude.

Paul now pleads with the Galatians in verse 15, "What then was the blessing you enjoyed?"

He asks them to remember back to their earlier response to the message. Now that they have listened to the Judaizers, have they turned against him? Has he become their enemy?

Sick and in pain, he had carried the good news at tremendous cost. He could have used his eye condition as an excuse not to preach to them, but he wanted them to know Jesus Christ. He wanted them to hear the good news. So he was willing to suffer to tell them of Jesus Christ, the Savior of the world.

"What has happened, dear Galatians?" he pleads as a pastor to his flock.

The Judaizers

In Galatians 4:17 Paul turns his attention to the Judaizers, telling his flock: "They zealously court you but not for good. Yes, they want to exclude you that you might be zealous for them."

Legalists win converts, not to Jesus Christ but to themselves. The Judaizers are zealous and determined. They work hard, not to lift up Christ, but to draw disciples to themselves so they can glory in attracting followers (Galatians 6:13). They are more concerned about their own pride and glory than about the Galatians' salvation.

Paul in Galatians 4:19 contrasts his own motivation with that of the Judaizers: "My little children, for whom I labor in birth again until Christ is formed in you."

A mother goes through a lot of pain when she delivers her children, but she rejoices as she holds her new child in her arms. Paul is saying, "I am like your mother. I was willing to go through all this terrible pain so that you could be found in Christ. And I remain in pain until you are totally established in Christ."

Christians at conversion change their citizenship from the world under Satan to heaven under Christ. But physically they remain in the world, so Christians are citizens of heaven living in enemy territory.

The apostle John in 1 John 5:19 says that the whole world—apart from believers—is under the evil one. When a person becomes a Christian Satan loses a subject, and he does his best to regain that person for his kingdom. One way he tries to destroy faith is by perverting the gospel, and this is what he did to the Galatians through the Judaizers. He cast a spell over them, as Galatians 3 brings out, and is now trying to deprive them of the joy of salvation in Christ.

Paul pleads with the Galatians to return to Christ. He will not let them go; he will continue working for them, pleading with them, until they are fully established in Christ.

He concludes this thought in verse 20: "I would like to be present with you now and to change my tone; for I have doubts about you."

Paul the Pastor

Paul wants to return to Galatia physically, but he has much to do. Travel is difficult. He wants to be with the Galatians when they turn back to Christ, for the power of legalism is strong.

Will they turn again to the pure gospel? He has his doubts, so he pleads with them to turn back to Christ as their only hope.

With great pain Paul first preached the gospel to the Galatians, ignoring his discomfort to bring them the good news of salvation. Now he is willing to go through the same pain all over again to restore them to Christ. These verses express the heart of Paul as he reflects God's *agape* (ah-GAH-pay) love.

In Romans 9:2 and 3 Paul expresses that same holy love toward his fellow Jews—men and women who now hate him and have turned against him. He says, "I am willing to be accursed that my own fellowmen should be saved."

Paul is not just a theologian; he is *the* theologian of the New Testament. But he has a pastor's heart and a great burden for those he has converted. He is not just an evangelist, establishing a church and then letting it fend for itself.

No, Paul is a pastor at heart. When he hears anything negative about those he has led to conversion, he writes them. "I wish I could use kinder words," he tells the Galatians, "but I am afraid that if I do, you may not realize the seriousness of your problem. So I am using these strong words that you, dear Galatians, will turn back to Jesus Christ as your one hundred percent Savior."

Galatianism Today

What Paul is saying to the Galatians is still true today. Christians are still living in enemy territory, where the devil can sidetrack them into legalism. Legalism is not something human beings must learn—it's inborn. If a pastor simply stops preaching the gospel, his flock will sooner or later take the road to legalism. Preachers must constantly teach the gospel in clarity to remind their flocks that salvation by performance is not possible.

Paul's burden for the Galatians applies to all Christians today. Paul, the great pastor, wants no one to be lost. As the devil has done through New Testament history, he uses legalism today to pull believers out of Christ. The book of Hebrews constantly reminds the Jewish Christian, "Please, don't go back to Judaism. Please don't go back to the legalism you were raised up with."

As we conclude this study, let us read from Hebrews 10 a companion passage to Galatians 4 meaningful to those trapped in legalism: "For you have need of endurance, so that after you have done the will of God, you may receive the promise."

Enduring Faith

Yes, justification is by faith alone, but Jesus Himself made it clear in Matthew 10:22 that faith must endure to the end. Hebrews 10:35 says in so many words, "Therefore do not cast away your confidence (in Christ), which has great reward, for you need to be patient. You need to endure unto the end. You need to cling to your faith until the reality of salvation takes place at the Second Coming of Christ."

The righteousness that qualifies believers for heaven, now and in the judgment, is always in Christ, *never in them*—not even in the righteousness God accomplishes *through them.* But the faith that makes the righteousness of Christ effective in their lives is not in heaven but *in them*. This faith can be touched; it can be destroyed. This is Satan's real purpose when he enters the Christian church and perverts the gospel. The writer of Hebrews says in verse 36: "For you have need of endurance, for after you have done the will of God (*God wants your faith to endure unto the end*), that you may receive the promise."

We have this promise brought out in verses 37 and 38: "For yet a little while and he who is coming will come and not tarry. Now, the just shall live by faith. But (*there is a "but" here*), if anyone draws back, my soul has no pleasure in him."

God is a God of love, and where there is love there can be no compulsion. As long as Christians believe, they are giving God the permission—the right—to take them to heaven because of the righteousness of Christ. Faith inherently contributes nothing toward their salvation, but it is an instrument—a channel—by which they receive the righteousness of Christ. The New Testament is absolutely clear that Christians are not saved *because* of their faith but *by* faith or *through* faith. Paul is saying to the Galatians, "Hold onto your faith. Turn back to Jesus Christ."

We read in Hebrews 10:39, "But we are not of those who draw back to perdition, but of those who believe to the saving of the soul." Belief in Jesus Christ as Savior is only the beginning; that faith must endure unto the end.

Writing in 2 Timothy 4:7, Paul says, "I have fought the fight. I have kept the faith." Paul is telling young Timothy that faith is a battle in the sense that one must hold fast to that faith until the end. The devil does everything he can to pull the Christian out of Christ, but as long as Christians recognize that they are 100 percent sinners, saved by grace, the devil cannot touch their faith.

Wrestling with Faith

Legalism, on the other hand, tells the believers that they possess merits that will recommend them for salvation. The believers first come to Christ, admitting that they are 100 percent sinners, and accept His righteousness. But after accepting Him, they come to believe that the good works they do contribute to their salvation—which is absolutely false. Salvation is either *all* through Christ or *not at all* through Him (Galatians 5:4).

It is my prayer that all who wrestle with their faith will endure to the very end. May they, like Paul, be able to say to God and their fellow believers: "I have fought the fight. I have kept the faith. Now, there is waiting for me, a crown of righteousness and not only for me, but for all that love His appearing."

Legalism is one of the gospel's greatest enemies and a great attraction to Christians. Believers must constantly remind themselves that they are, by nature and performance, 100 percent sinners and that their self-righteousness is worthless.

Yes, through the Holy Spirit performance may include many righteous works, but these righteous works make no contribution to their salvation. Even if a Christian has not committed a single selfish, sinful act for, say, the past two hours, they are still sinners by nature during those two hours.

God so loved the world that He sent His only begotten Son, not to condemn sinners, but that they through His doing and dying could be saved (John 3:17).

May those who believe never allow anything—anybody, any philosophy—to pull them out of Christ. May they be on guard against legalism, even in subtle forms and religious garb, that they may not be deceived.

May those who know and accept the truth constantly hold onto it and when Christ comes, may they be able to cry with great jubilation, "This is my God, I have been waiting for Him." Man's only hope is Jesus Christ and His righteousness. Justification is by faith alone.

Chapter 10
The Two Covenants
Galatians 4:21-31

Many consider Galatians 4:21-31 to be the epistle's most difficult passage for modern readers. The reasons for these difficulties are threefold.

First, Paul presupposes that his readers know their Old Testament well—something few Christians do today. Second, Paul's argument in this passage is somewhat technical—familiar to the rabbinical schools of his day but not to 21st-century Christians.

Finally, this passage poses difficulty for those who limit the terms "Old Covenant" and "New Covenant" to time—who believe that the Old Covenant refers only to the period of history from Moses to Christ; the New Covenant to the period of time from the cross to the end of time.

According to the New Testament—especially Paul—the terms "Old" and "New" covenants actually have two applications—historical as well as theological.

Historical and Theological Covenants

The terms Old Covenant and New Covenant historically have to do with time. When God gave the law through Moses, sinful humanity came legally under the law and its curse. This is historically the "Old Covenant." That curse was lifted when Christ came and redeemed mankind some 1,500 years later (New Covenant). We know this from our study of Galatians 3:23-25 and Hebrews 8:7-13.

But these two covenants also have a theological meaning. When these terms are used in the theological sense, the Old

Covenant refers to salvation by works. In contrast the New Covenant refers to salvation by grace. Both covenants, then, are timeless in a theological sense.

If you and I today were to promise God that we will be good and keep the commandments in order to be saved, we would be entering into an Old Covenant agreement, or contract. It is in this theological sense—this second sense—that Paul deals with the two terms in Galatians 4:21-31.

Let us now study this passage, where Paul makes a three-step argument—beginning with the first step in verses 21-23.

Paul's Argument

Paul begins his argument by citing the names Ishmael and Isaac, two sons of the patriarch Abraham. Second he uses these two sons in verses 24-27 as symbols of the two methods of salvation: salvation by keeping the law (salvation by works), identified with the Old Covenant and its bondage; and salvation by grace (the New Covenant), a religion of freedom, joy, peace and hope.

Finally, in verses 28-31 Paul applies the arguments to his readers—the Galatians and, by extension, Christians of all time. Judaism is a religion of bondage, he says, since the law condemns sinners. But true Christianity is a religion of freedom, since Christ redeemed mankind from the curse of the law (see Galatians 3:13).

Let's read Galatians 4:21-30 and follow Paul's three-step argument: "Tell me, you who desire to be under the law, do you not hear the law? For it is written that Abraham had two sons: the one by a bond-woman, the other by a free-woman. But he who was of the bond-woman was born according to the flesh, and he of the free-woman through promise, which things are symbolic. For these are the two covenants: the one from Mount Sinai which gives birth to bondage, which is Hagar (that is, the mother of

Ishmael) for this Hagar is Mount Sinai in Arabia, and corresponds to Jerusalem which now is, and is in bondage with her children. But the Jerusalem above is free, which is the mother of us all. For it is written: 'Rejoice, O barren, you who do not bear! Break forth and shout, You who do not travail! For the desolate has many more children Than she who had a husband.' Now, we brethren, as Isaac was, are children of promise. But, as he who was born according to the flesh then persecuted him who was born according to the Spirit, even so it is now. Nevertheless, what does the Scripture say? 'Cast out the bondwoman and her son, for the son of the bondwoman shall not be heir with the son of the freewoman.'"

Under the Law

What does Paul mean in verse 21 when he writes, "Tell me you who desire to be under the law." Some believe "under the law" means that a person is cursed. Yes, if a sinner is under the law a curse results, but "under law" simply means that one is ruled by the law and lives under its dominion.

A person under law must then justify himself before God on the basis of his performance, or righteousness. In other words, Paul is saying, "Tell me, you who desire to be saved—you who desire to earn your salvation through the keeping of the law—don't you hear what the law says?"

The word "law" here refers to the Torah, the first five books of the Old Testament written by Moses and often referred to as the Pentateuch.

Meshing the Testaments

Paul now refers us to the history of Abraham and his two sons, recorded in Genesis. Abraham had two sons—the first Ishmael, which he produced through a servant woman named Hagar, and the second Isaac, which God gave him and his aged wife Sarah through a special miracle.

Galatians 4:23 tells us, "But he who was of the bondwoman was born according to the flesh and he of the freewoman through promise."

Unless one is familiar with the Old Testament story of Abraham, the application seems meaningless. Too many Christians unfortunately ignore the Old Testament, forgetting that the Old and New Testaments are a unit. The Old is the promise, the New is the reality.

Abraham's History

The story as paraphrased from Genesis 12 and onwards says that when Abraham is about 75 years old God tells him, "I want you to leave your home, neighbors, and family (all of whom are idol worshipers [Joshua 24:2]). I want you to go to the land that I will give you (which we know today as the land of Israel) and I will make you a great nation."

Abraham is 75 years old at that time and his wife, Sarah, is 65, but they have no children. But God promises Abraham a son and Abraham believes God and is counted righteous.

A year goes by. Two years go by. Three years go by. In fact, eight years go by and there is no child! Abraham begins to doubt God's promise. So God comes again to Abraham and asks (paraphrasing Genesis 15), "Why are you fearful? Why have you begun to doubt My promise?"

Again paraphrasing, Abraham responds, "God, it takes nine months for human beings to produce a child. How long does it take You? Eight years have now passed. Look at this boy in my home, the son of my slave Eleazer. Is this the promised son or am I to look for another son?"

"Come, Abraham, let's go for a walk," God responds. The area where Abraham lives in Palestine has little rain. The night sky is clear. God says, "Abraham, count the stars."

"Impossible," says Abraham. "There are too many."

God answers, "This is how many children you will have. The son I promise you is not the son of a slave. The son I promise will come from your own loins. He will be your child, not somebody else's."

Then we read in Genesis 15:6 those famous words Paul loves to quote, "Abraham believed God and he was counted righteous."

Abraham is now 83 years old, but his faith is restored. But God delays some more—not one or two years but 13 or 14 years—until Sarah passes the age of childbearing. Physically and scientifically Sarah can no longer bear children, and God asks again, "Abraham, now do you still believe I can give you a child?"

Ishmael

Before we look at Abraham's answer, however, we need to study Genesis 16, where we find a story that takes place just two years after God tells Abraham his descendants will be as the stars.

The 75-year-old Sarah now comes to her 85-year-old husband and says, "It's now impossible for God to give you a child through me. He said 'your loins' but He mentioned nothing about me. Abraham, it's time you helped God keep His promise. Why don't you take my slave girl, Hagar, as my surrogate and produce a child and help God out?" Abraham accepts Sarah's advice and he and Hagar produce a son, Ishmael.

Now, more than 10 years after Ishmael's birth, Sarah has definitely passed the age of childbearing and God comes again to Abraham and asks, "Do you believe I can still give you a child through Sarah?"

In Romans 4:17 and onward Paul tells us that against hope—against all rational evidence—Abraham believes God. Abraham takes God at His word, and one year later Sarah bears a baby boy and they name him Isaac—which means "laughter", or rejoicing.

Ishmael is now approximately 13 years old, and one day Sarah hears Ishmael making fun of Isaac. So she goes to Abraham and says, "Abraham, I want you to get rid of this woman and her son. I do not want this son of hers to share the inheritance that my son, Isaac, is going to have."

Sarah (who came up with the idea of a surrogate birth in the first place) has turned against the young man. Abraham is deeply concerned, for though Ishmael is not *Sarah's* child, he *is* Abraham's firstborn son.

Distressed, Abraham turns to God for advice and God tells him in so many words, "Abraham, Sarah is right this time. You have to get rid of this surrogate mother and her son, Ishmael. The promise that I made to you, 'In thy seed shall all nations be blessed' has to be fulfilled through Isaac. Ishmael has no part in this plan" (see Genesis 21:8-12).

Paul uses these two Old Testament children as symbols of the two methods of salvation (covenants)—salvation by works (Ishmael) and salvation by faith in Jesus Christ (Isaac).

Sinai and the New Jerusalem

With this in mind let us return to Galatians 4:24. Ishmael and Isaac are symbolic of two covenants. The first was made at Mount Sinai and gives birth to bondage. The law does nothing to save, but it does curse those who break it. This is the Old Covenant.

Paul then tells us that Hagar, representing Mount Sinai, also represents the earthly Jerusalem, where the Jews are still under Roman bondage when Paul writes this letter. He tells the Galatians that Judaism of his day is still in bondage to legalism.

But in verse 26 Paul explains that the Jerusalem from above—that is, the heavenly Jerusalem—is free and is the mother of all Christians (the "us all" refers to the believers, born-again Christians). Then Paul quotes Isaiah 54:1, "Rejoice O barren, you who do not bear."

All human beings are sinners. All are incapable of producing any righteousness. We are barren when it comes to salvation by works. (This is theologically the Old Covenant—and it's timeless.) But Paul tells us by quoting Isaiah 54 that we should rejoice because we who were desolate have now had more children than those who have husbands. The gospel brings rejoicing and hope.

He then says all Christians, like Isaac, are "children of promise," not of human working or striving. (This is theologically the New Covenant and is also timeless.)

Those who try to reach heaven by their own performance are children of Ishmael. Those who put their faith in Jesus Christ for the gift of God's promised salvation are children of Isaac.

But now let us go one step further. God mentions in the Bible many times that the Jews have three fathers—Abraham, Isaac and Jacob. The Jews have concluded that only those who are physical, literal descendants of these three men can belong to God's covenant people and receive salvation.

But such an interpretation entirely perverts what God intended when He gave Israel three fathers. Paul—a Jew himself—corrects this in Romans 9:6-8 and makes it clear that not everyone who is a child of Abraham belongs to Israel. Not everyone who claims Abraham, Isaac, and Jacob as ancestors is a true Jew.

What these three fathers *do* symbolize is the set of basic traits that genuine Christians all possess: Abraham stands for faith (Romans 4:16 and 17; Galatians 3:8 and 9), Isaac means "born from above" (Galatians 4:28), and Israel (Jacob) stands for endurance (Jeremiah 30:7).

To be children of God we must have the faith of Abraham, the new birth of Isaac, and the endurance of Jacob.

Symbols Applied

Now let us look at the application of these two symbols—Isaac and Ishmael. In verse 29 Paul tells us, "Nevertheless, what does the Scripture say?"

This question is based on the observation he makes in verse

28: "Now, we brethren, as Isaac was, are children of promise. But as he who was born according to the flesh, then persecuted him who was born according to the Spirit, even so it is now."

Paul is saying in verse 29 that just as Ishmael made life miserable for Isaac, so Satan will make life miserable for those who stand under the grace of God. To become a Christian means to face persecution. Why? Because as already mentioned, a Christian belongs to the kingdom of Heaven but is still living in enemy territory. The enemy will make sure that life is miserable for them, hoping that they will give up their faith in Christ. In this case Satan uses legalism.

Paul advises his hearers in verse 30: "Nevertheless what does the Scripture say? Cast out the bondwoman and her son for the son of the bondwoman shall not be heir with the son of the freewoman."

Salvation by works of the law and salvation by grace are mutually exclusive. They cannot be merged; they cannot marry. There can be no synthesis. It's one or the other. And those who believe in Jesus Christ—who are justified by faith—must cast out any legalism or legalistic tendency they may have inherited or may be clinging to from their past.

As Paul says in Philippians 3:7-9, Christians must take all their self-righteousness and count it but dung that they may win Christ and salvation through faith in Him alone.

Christians simply cannot be justified by faith *plus* other virtues. The moment they add *anything* to salvation by grace, Paul tells us in Galatians 5:4 that they fall from grace and Christ becomes of *no effect* to them. The Old and New Covenants theologically cannot be synthesized.

May this study from Galatians 4:21-31 convince every Christian reader beyond any doubt that salvation comes by grace alone, through faith alone, because of Christ alone. May they reject anything that leans toward legalism and remind themselves daily that they are 100 percent sinners, saved by faith in Jesus Christ and His righteousness.

May they know the truth, cling to it, and endure unto the end, is my prayer.

Chapter 11
Freedom in Christ

Galatians 5:1-12

Paul's whole purpose in writing to the Galatian Christians is to restore them to freedom and peace in Christ. The Judaizers have deceived and trapped these Galatian Christians into a subtle form of legalism and robbed them of the joy of salvation.

Having shown them their error from every conceivable angle, Paul now gives these Galatians some practical counsel. In Galatians 5:1-12 Paul contrasts the two methods of salvation—salvation by grace alone versus salvation by works of the law. The way of grace and the way of the law are mutually exclusive to Paul. The way of law makes salvation dependent on human achievement, but the person who takes the way of grace simply casts himself and his sins upon the mercy of God. This is the distinction between the Old and New Covenants theologically.

The two ways cannot be combined; they are diametrically opposed to each other. In Galatians 5:1-12 Paul draws the contrast twice—first, in verses 1-6, from the standpoint of those who practice these two methods, and again in verses 7-12, from the standpoint of those who preach them.

We read: "Stand fast therefore in the liberty by which Christ has made us free, and do not be entangled again with a yoke of bondage. Indeed I, Paul, say to you that if you become circumcised, Christ will profit you nothing. And I testify again to every man who becomes circumcised that he is a debtor to keep the whole law. You have become estranged from Christ, you who attempt to be justified by law; you have fallen from grace. For we through the Spirit eagerly wait for the hope of righteousness by faith. For in Christ Jesus neither circumcision nor uncircumcision avails anything, but faith working through love. You ran well. Who hindered you from obeying the truth? This persuasion does not come from Him who calls you. A little leaven leavens the whole lump. I have confidence in you, in the Lord, that you will have no other mind; but he who troubles you shall bear his judgment whoever he is. And I, brethren, if I still preach circumcision, why do I still suffer persecution? Then the offense of the cross has ceased. I could wish that those who trouble you would even cut themselves off!"

Freedom from the Law

We find in verse 1 that Paul gives two commands to the Galatian Christians. He has convinced them that man's only hope is in salvation by grace through faith in Jesus Christ. Now he says, "Stand fast therefore, in the liberty by which Christ has made us free." He wants them to stand firm in their freedom. Freedom from what? Freedom from being under the law.

We read in Galatians 4:4 and 5 that when the fullness of time came, Christ was sent by the Father, made of a woman, made under the law. Why? "To redeem us from under the law that we may receive the adoption of sons."

In Galatians 3:10 Paul says that anyone under the law is under a curse because the law curses everyone whose performance is not perfect. Having explained the gospel to the Galatians and defended it from every angle, Paul says in Galatians 5:1 to stand fast in their liberty. He pleads with them not to go back to legalism, which he defines as the yoke of bondage.

First Major Controversy

The question of legalism is one of the first major controversies the early Christian church faces. Acts 15 describes the first Jerusalem Council—the first general church council—, which was convened specifically to deal with the issue of legalism. The same Judaizers are apparently there, insisting that the Galatian Christians be circumcised. We read what they say in Acts 15:1: "Unless you are circumcised according to the custom of Moses, you cannot be saved."

They add in verse 5, "It is necessary to circumcise them and to command them to keep the law of Moses."

In other words, "They have to keep all the rules, all the 'dos' and 'don'ts' described in the first five books of Moses in the Old Testament if they want to be saved. It is not enough just to believe; they must keep the law besides in order to be saved."

This teaching by the Judaizers produces a tremendous controversy, for we read in Acts 15:2: "Therefore, when Paul and Barnabas had no small dissension and dispute with them (*the Judaizers*), they determined that Paul and Barnabas and certain others of them, should go up to Jerusalem to the apostles and elders about this question." And so the first Jerusalem Council is called.

Peter summarizes the conclusion of the Council with these words in Acts 15:10 and 11: "Now, therefore, why do you test God by putting a yoke on the necks of the disciples which neither our fathers nor we were able to bear?"

Addressing the Judaizers, Peter asks, "Why are you asking the Gentiles to accept legal requirements that neither our fathers nor we could satisfy? Why are you going back to this yoke of bondage?"

He concludes in verse 11: "But we (*the apostles)* believe that through the grace of the Lord, Jesus Christ, we (*Jews*) shall be saved in the same manner as they (*Gentiles*)."

Salvation for sinners comes only through the grace of the Lord, Jesus Christ. But the apostles are absolutely united on the question of how mankind is saved. Salvation comes by grace alone—in the doing and the dying of Jesus Christ.

An Easy Yoke

Now in Galatians 5:1, Paul pleads in so many words: "Please, don't go back to this yoke of bondage." The yoke of bondage is slavery and a slave lives in constant fear of his master's strictness. In contrast to this yoke of bondage, Jesus Himself introduces a different kind of yoke in Matthew 11:28 and 29.

Speaking to Jews who fear they are not good enough to be saved, Jesus shares this good news: "Come to me, all you who labor (*are striving to earn salvation*) and are heavy laden (*living under fear, guilt, and distress*) and I will give you rest. Take my yoke upon you and learn from Me. . . ."

This is not the yoke of legalism. This is the yoke of Christ, who says, ". . . for I am gentle and lowly in heart and you will find rest for your souls, for my yoke is easy and my burden is light."

What is this yoke of Christ? Jesus states clearly, "I do nothing of Myself. I live by the father. The works that I do, it is not I, but the Father who dwells in Me. He is the One who does the works" (John 8:28). The yoke of Christ is to live lives totally dependent on God—that is, by faith alone. In contrast, the yoke of bondage is a yoke that depends totally on a Christian's performance.

Paul is telling the Galatians, in so many words, "You took the yoke of Christ, which is the yoke of total God-dependence and brings peace, hope, joy, and assurance because God has redeemed us in Jesus Christ. But you have gone back to the yoke of bondage. Please, don't be fools. Hold on to your yoke of Christ which has set you free, free from guilt, free from condemnation, free from the curse of the law."

This beautiful statement, found in Hebrews 10:19-23, deals with the same issue: "Therefore, brethren, having boldness to enter the Holiest (*the very presence of God*) by the blood of Jesus, by a new and living way (*unlike the legalism of their earlier lives)* which he (*Christ*) consecrated for us through the veil that is his flesh and having a High Priest over the house of God. . ."

The book of Hebrews was written to Jewish Christians who, like the Galatians, are in danger of reverting to legalism. In the Old Testament sanctuary, a veil separated the Holy Place from the Most Holy Place. The ministering priest who functioned daily in the Holy Place was himself a sinner and required this protection from the presence of God.

In contrast, the writer of Hebrews says to the believing Jews, "Let us draw near (*to God*) with a true heart with a full assurance of faith having our hearts sprinkled from an evil conscience and our bodies washed with pure water. Let us hold fast the confession of our hope without wavering for He who promised is faithful."

To both the Hebrews and the Galatians Paul is saying, "Stand fast, therefore, in the liberty by which Christ has made us free."

After Paul exhorts the Galatians to "Stand fast," he follows up with a second—a negative—command in Galatians 5:1, part two: "Do not be entangled again with the yoke of bondage." The yoke of bondage, as we have seen, is legalism.

Estrangement from Christ

Now in Galatians 5:2, he says, "Indeed I, Paul, say to you that if you become circumcised, Christ will profit you nothing." Salvation by grace and salvation by law keeping are two diametrically opposite systems of salvation, he says. Paul is not against circumcision and in fact circumcised Timothy. But he is against circumcision when it is used as a method of salvation. Those who become circumcised in order to be saved, he says, are placing themselves under the law. And since the law—the Torah—is a unit, those under the law are obligated to keep every single requirement of the law in order to be saved.

In verse 4, now, Paul says: "You have become estranged from Christ (*you have turned your back on Christ*), you who attempt to be justified by law: you have fallen from grace."

It is not enough to know the law. It is not enough to keep part of the law. It is not even enough to keep most of the law. Those who depend on the law for salvation and fail to keep the law in even one point have failed completely (James 2:10).

The moment a Christian adds law keeping as a requirement for salvation, he or she falls from grace, for the two methods of salvation—legalism versus grace—are diametrically opposed. They cannot be mixed. They are mutually exclusive. To turn to the law as a means of salvation is to say good-bye to salvation by grace.

Paul says in 1 Timothy 1:15 that Christ came to save sinners and that those who regard the law as a means of salvation are denying their total depravity as sinful humans. To strive for salvation through obedience to the law is to deny one's need for grace.

Ultimate Salvation

Paul now says in Galatians 5:5, "For we through the Spirit eagerly wait for the hope of righteousness by faith."

When Christians accept Christ, the Holy Spirit comes and dwells in them and they become born-again. Paul says in Romans 8:16 and 17 that the first thing the Holy Spirit does is to convince them that they are God's children. He brings with Him peace from Jesus Christ and Him crucified.

Though baptized believers stand justified before God in Christ, they still have sinful natures. They still live in a sinful world, and salvation as an ultimate reality is still future. Yes, they are saved by hope, Paul says in Romans 8:24 and 25, but hope would not be hope if there were nothing left to hope for.

Three-part Salvation

Because Christians are saved by hope, they patiently wait for glorification, for Jesus Christ promises a three-part salvation, subjectively.

First comes *justification,* which means to stand perfect—to stand completely righteous—before God and His law in Christ Jesus. The moment human beings accept salvation through Christ, the law no longer condemns them (Romans 8:1). They have passed from death to life. These are the words of Jesus in John 5:24. But though their standing before God is perfect, they still have sinful natures.

The second element of salvation is an ongoing, daily process in the Christian experience known as *sanctification*. Through the Spirit the flesh is conquered. In Galatians 5:16 Paul says, "Walk in the Spirit and you will not fulfill the lusts of the flesh." This is sanctification. But Christian growth through holy living does nothing to change a Christian's inherently sinful nature.

The third and final element of salvation is *glorification*. This takes place at the Second Coming of Christ, when this corruption puts on incorruption and this mortal puts on immortality (1 Corinthians 15:50-54). Then—and then only—will Christians experience the total salvation they have accepted in Jesus Christ by faith (Romans 5:1). Paul is saying that a true Christian has peace with God through justification by faith, but Christians must patiently wait for ultimate salvation when their bodies themselves are redeemed (Romans 8:22-25). When it comes to salvation as an experience, the New Testament uses all three word tenses—past, present, and future—so a Christian from the moment of conversion must say, "I am saved" (justification), "I am being saved" (sanctification), and "I will be saved" (glorification).

In Galatians 5:6 Paul says that in Christ Jesus neither circumcision nor non-circumcision avails anything. Salvation is entirely a free gift. What Christians do—whether through the act of circumcision or the act of baptism—adds nothing to their salvation. Any performance done in the name of Christ does not save them—even casting out devils and performing miracles.

Yes, sanctification is the evidence *of* justification. It is the fruit *of* salvation, but makes no contribution *to* salvation. Anything the

Christian does or God does through the Christian has no saving merit. Christians are saved entirely by Jesus Christ and Him crucified.

True Jews

In other words Paul is saying, "You Galatian Christians, if you are trying to become Jews through the circumcision, you are deceiving yourselves. The only true Jew in God's eyes is a Jew who has no confidence in himself and is resting in Christ."

Christians are saved only one way—Jew or Gentile—it happens only through the life, death, and resurrection of Jesus Christ.

The only behavioral result of genuine justification is faith that works through love. The moment Christians accept Christ, the Holy Spirit comes and dwells in them, reminding them that they are children of God and bringing peace to their hearts. But the Holy Spirit also brings a vital ingredient into the Christian life known as *agape* (ah-GAH-pay) love. Paul describes *agape* in detail in 1 Corinthians 13 and identifies it as the supreme gift of the Holy Spirit to the believer. This *agape* love seeks not her own. It is not proud. It is not boastful. It is a love that was revealed in the life of Christ and loves its neighbors more than itself. It is a love that reflects the character of Christ, and while Christians await glorification, this love will be growing in their hearts.

Reflecting Jesus

In the Sermon on the Mount (Matthew 5:14) Jesus tells his disciples, "You are the light of the world."

The "you" is plural in the original and the word "light" is singular, for the Light represents only one Person—Jesus Christ (John 8:12). But as the Spirit of Christ indwells the Christian, Christ is reflected more and more in them. Jesus says in Matthew 5:16, "Let this light (*let Christ*) shine out of you by your good works." As Jesus did, so the Christian will go about doing good.

In John 13:34 and 35 Jesus makes it clear that if Christians love one another as Christ loved them (the fruit of salvation), they will be recognized as His disciples because of their *agape* love one for another. This is Christianity in action.

Running the Race

In Galatians 5:7 Paul says, "You ran well. Who hindered you from obeying the truth?"

What an important statement: "You ran well." Salvation is a gift—it requires no "running." It is free. But Christian living is like a race and requires much effort, as Christians walk in the Spirit by faith, enduring to the end. Jesus says in Matthew 10:17-22, "He who endures unto the end will be saved."

In Hebrews 10:35-39 the writer of Hebrews tells the Jewish Christians: "He who draws back from justification by faith will end up in perdition, but he whose faith endures unto the end will rejoice when Christ comes."

Leavening the Lump

Those who enter the shelter of justification by faith now must battle against unbelief. In verse 9 Paul says that a little leavening expands the whole lump. What does he mean?

In Matthew 16:5-12 the words of Jesus help us understand Paul's words. Jesus has traveled to the less-populated side of the Sea of Galilee, but his disciples have failed to bring along any food. There are no shops where they can buy bread, and the disciples tell the Lord, "We have no bread."

Jesus responds, "Beware of the leaven of the Pharisees and Sadducees."

The disciples believe he is talking about the bread they have forgotten to bring along, but Jesus sets the record straight, telling them in so many words: "No, I am not referring to bread. Don't you remember how I took three loaves and five fishes and fed 5,000? Why are you of so little faith?"

The disciples then realize that He is not talking of physical bread but about legalism. He is saying, in so many words, "Legalism is extremely dangerous." The moment a little legalism creeps into the church, it affects the whole body. Legalism must be fought with everything the church possesses.

Paul says in Galatians 5:10, "I have confidence in you in the Lord that you will have no other mind." He is appealing to them, saying in so many words, "I believe you are not fools. I believe this false teaching will not deceive you. I believe you will realize your mistake and return to Christ."

He then continues, "But he who troubled you *(Satan, through the Judaizers)* shall bear his judgment for whoever he is." Paul already has told them in Galatians 1:8 and 9: "Anyone who preaches another gospel other than what was preached by the apostles, let him be accursed."

Now, in Galatians 5:11 and 12, Paul says, "I, brethren, if I still preach circumcision, why do I still suffer persecution? Then the offense of the cross has ceased. I would wish that those who trouble you would even cut themselves off (*mutilate or castrate themselves*)!"

What does Paul mean by *the offence of the cross*? The cross is God's verdict on the flesh (sinful nature). As Christ implied in John 3:6, the flesh will always remain flesh. It cannot be salvaged but only crucified (Galatians 5:24). To those who glory in self-righteousness the cross is therefore offensive.

Paul is very direct here, for he realizes that legalism is one of the greatest enemies of the gospel. He does not want any of the Galatians to be sidetracked from the true gospel of Jesus Christ. This is equally true for Christians living in the 21st century.

Chapter 12
True Christian Freedom

Galatians 5:13-15

While I was working as a missionary in Uganda, a young Ugandan once approached me with a question: "Are you saved?"

He clearly did not realize who I was and, bless his heart, he wanted to witness for Jesus Christ. So I responded, "Saved from what?"

"Are you saved from sin?" he challenged.

"Can you be more specific?" I asked. "Are you asking about guilt and punishment of sin, the slavery and power of sin, or the nature and the presence of sin? Which one?"

He looked at me for a long time and said, "You sound like a pastor."

"Yes, I am a pastor," I told him. "In fact, I am a missionary to your country. Can I ask you the same question? Are you saved?"

With great enthusiasm, his arms lifted in the air, he shouted, "Yes, I'm saved. I was saved three months ago."

"Then what on earth are you doing here if you are already saved?" I asked him.

As we studied last chapter, the Christian can indeed say, "I am saved," but should never stop there. The Christian is "saved (justified), being saved (sanctified), and will be saved (glorified)." But the conversation with the young African man continued, as I challenged him, "If you are saved, why do I smell beer on your breath?"

He turned to me and said, "Pastor, you know we are saved by grace and not by what we do."

"Oh," I said, "you mean to say that Christ lived a perfect life for us?"

"Yes!" he said.

"And He died instead of us?"

"Now you have it!" the young man said, excited.

"No," I said, "there's one more step."

"What's that?" he asked

"He also went to heaven instead of you," I said.

Oh, he didn't like that! But he had a New Testament in his pocket and I asked him to please read 2 Timothy 2:11: "If we are to live with Christ, we must first die with Him."

Cheap Grace

I asked the young man to read the passage because he had turned freedom in Christ into license. In church history, wherever the true gospel is proclaimed, some abuse their freedom in Christ. A famous German martyr, Dietrich Bonhoffer, calls this cheap grace. Legalism is the enemy of the gospel, but the danger of the gospel is antinomianism, or cheap grace.

Paul is fully aware of this problem and spends all of Romans 6 dealing with it. Shall we keep on sinning because we are under grace, because grace abounds? Paul answers, "God forbid" (verses 1 and 2).

Shall we keep on sinning because we are not under the law but under grace? He answers, "It is unthinkable. God forbid" (verses 14 and 15).

Paul shares this very concern in Galatians 5:13-15, for two reasons: First, there is danger that these Galatians will swing from legalism directly to antinomianism; and second, the Judaizers constantly accuse Paul of promoting cheap grace.

The Judaizers claim, in so many words, "If you tell the world—if you tell Christians—that they already stand justified in Christ (Romans 5:1), are perfect in Christ, are complete in Him (Colossians 2:10), and have already passed from death to life (John 5:24), you have removed all incentive for them to live holy lives."

Four Christian Freedoms

As we turn to Galatians 5:13-15, we ask ourselves, "How are we, then, to define true Christian freedom?"

Foremost, we must understand the bondage from which the good news of the gospel sets Christians free. Only then can we understand what Christian freedom *is not*.

In Galatians 5:1-12 (studied last chapter) Paul reminds the Galatian Christians that Christ has set them free and that they must not allow anyone to rob them of this freedom. What *is* this freedom in Christ?

Scripture tells us of four areas of freedom. *First*, Christ sets the believers free from all condemnation. Romans 8:1 makes a wonderful statement in context of the Christian's struggle to live a holy life: "There is therefore now no condemnation for those who are in Christ Jesus." In Christ Jesus those who believe are set free from the condemnation of the law and its curse.

The *second* freedom Christ offers is freedom from the fear of death. The wages of sin is death—eternal death. But Hebrews 2:14 and 15 says: "Inasmuch then as the children have partaken of flesh and blood, He Himself likewise (*referring to Christ*) shared in the same, that through death he might destroy him who had the power of death, that is, the devil, and release those who through fear of death, were all their lifetime subject to bondage."

Every human being is born a slave to the fear of death. In war, it is said, there are no atheists in foxholes. Jesus came to set mankind free from this fear of death through his life, death, and resurrection. He did this because of love—God's unconditional love for the world.

In 1 John 4:16-18 we read that perfect knowledge of God's love and His redeeming activity in Christ removes fear of the judgment. Christians in the early church and more recently Christians in communist countries became renowned for their willingness to die for their faith. Why? Because they knew in whom they believed and had the hope of the resurrection.

Third, Christ sets the believers free from their slavery to sin. Sin is not only an act, it is a force. It is a power that dwells within human nature. Paul brings this out clearly in Romans 7:14, where he says that the law is spiritual but human beings are carnal, sold as slaves to sin.

Jesus Himself speaks of this freedom in John 8:32-36. Addressing the Jews, he says: "And you shall know the truth and the truth shall make you free."

Free? Free from what? "We are Abraham's descendants and have never been in bondage to anyone," the Jews claim. "How can you say, 'You will be made free?'"

How the Jews can claim this, given their bondage to Rome in Jesus' day, is beside the point. But Jesus answers them, "Most assuredly I say to you, whoever commits sin is a slave of sin."

Jesus is not talking about political freedom. He is talking about mankind's slavery to sin, for he says in verses 35 and 36, "And a slave does not abide in the house forever but a son abides forever. Therefore, if the son makes you free, you shall be free indeed."

Christ, the Son, sets those who believe in Him free from the slavery to sin. In Romans 6:18 and 22 Paul says that Christians who have been set free from sin live holy lives and in the end receive eternal life.

The *fourth* area of freedom in Christ is freedom from the jurisdiction of the law. In Romans 6:14 Paul tells the believers, "Sin shall no longer have dominion over you because you are not under the law but under grace."

Paul says in Romans 3:19 that the whole world stands condemned—guilty under the law. But in Romans 6:14, he tells believers that they are no longer under law but under grace. Clearly, one of the freedoms a Christian receives is deliverance from being "under law" to being "under grace."

The law can no longer say to the believer, "Obey and live; if you disobey, you will die." The Christian no longer lives under that system. He is under grace, and grace brings salvation, based on the doing and dying of the Lord, Jesus Christ.

These are the four areas of true Christian freedom: Freedom from (1) the condemnation of sin, (2) fear of death, (3) slavery to sin, and (4) the jurisdiction of the law.

Free to Sin?

The gospel, however, in no way frees the Christian to sin. In the heart of every human being is an inborn desire for freedom—political freedom, economic freedom, social freedom, and spiritual freedom. Most world news on television today springs directly or indirectly from mankind's desire for, or pursuit of, freedom.

Mankind cannot save itself spiritually; it is bankrupt. But too often, when freedom arrives in Christ, human beings misunderstand and misuse this freedom.

An experience I had in Kenya illustrates how this can happen. One day while taking my wife to the African market, I saw a group of old men, handcuffed and guarded by a policeman. So while my wife was doing the shopping, I decided to visit and comfort these prisoners.

I had no idea what crime they had committed, so I said to them in Swahili, "Why are you in handcuffs? What is your problem?"

One of the older men replied, "When is independence coming to an end?" He meant independence from British rule.

"Coming to an end!" I exclaimed. "No, your freedom now is permanent. You have obtained independence."

The old man then told me that when Kenya had been a British colony, the British government had been somewhat lax in collecting taxes from national Africans. If they failed to pay the tax, the British might simply require them to work off the tax by maintaining the road in front of their houses.

But as the Kenyans fought for freedom, many thought that freedom from British rule would mean freedom from all taxes. So now these poor Africans were in handcuffs for failing to pay their tax, and I explained to them that having independence requires responsibility.

"How on earth do you expect the president and government to run the country without money, and how are they to get money if they don't charge you tax?" I asked.

Likewise Christianity, which sets the believers free in so many ways, does not set them free to do as they please.

New Morality

Some years ago American society began loosening many traditional restrictions and gave people more personal freedom—freedom often referred to as the "New Morality."

But since mankind is a slave to sin, this freedom has created endless problems. Premarital sex has grown, abortions have increased, and crime has reached such a point that many theologians became desperate to offer a solution.

They came up with a plan known as "Reconstruction Theology," in which the Christian community campaigns to place their own in powerful national offices where they can legislate morality.

What they forget is that morality cannot be legislated—legalism cannot elevate the moral tone of a people. Other governments have tried this approach and all have fallen into deep, bureaucratic corruption. The only way man can be set free from his slavery to sin is through the gospel of the Lord, Jesus Christ.

From Legalism to Cheap Grace

Paul is aware of the Galatians' temptation to move from legalism to cheap grace, or antinomianism. In Galatians 5:13-15 he tells them what Christian freedom *is not*: "For you, brethren, have been called to liberty, only do not use liberty as an opportunity for the flesh but through love, serve one another. For all the law is fulfilled in one word, even in this, You shall love your neighbor as yourself. But if you bite and devour one another, beware lest you be consumed by one another."

First, Paul says in the first part of verse 13, Christian freedom is not freedom to indulge the flesh: "For you, brethren, have been called to liberty, only do not use liberty as an opportunity for the flesh. . . . "

Second, Christian freedom does not give license to exploit fellow believers. Instead, Paul says, "serve one another." The gospel gives no license to live according to the flesh or to exploit fellow human beings.

A case in point arose among the Thessalonians in Paul's day. Many Thessalonian Christians believed Christ was coming soon, so they stopped cultivating their gardens and began imposing on their fellow believers for food.

Paul says to them in 2 Thessalonians 3:6-9: "But we command you, brethren, in the name of our Lord Jesus Christ that you withdraw from every brother who walks disorderly and not according to the tradition which he received from us. For you yourselves know how you ought to follow us for we were not disorderly among you nor did we eat anyone's bread free of charge but worked with labor and toil night and day that we might not be a burden to any of you, not because we do not have authority, but to make ourselves an example of how you should follow us. For even when we were with you, we commanded you this, If anyone will not work, neither shall he eat."

Too many take advantage of Christian love and hospitality. Paul says, in so many words, "Don't allow that to happen. Christians must serve one another, but if anyone begins taking advantage of this charity, the counsel of 2 Thessalonians 3:6-10 applies to them." Christian freedom is not freedom to exploit fellow believers, simply because they happen to possess wealth.

Third, Christian freedom does not give license to disregard

God's law. Many Christians mistakenly believe that Paul opposes God's law. Paul never speaks against the law—only against its misuse as a method of salvation.

Paul always upholds the law as a standard of Christian living. The law—especially the spirit of the law, which is love—must be upheld as a standard of Christian living but condemned as a means of salvation.

The Spirit of the Law

Galatians 5:14 says: "For all the law is fulfilled in one word even in this, 'You shall love your neighbor as yourself.'"

Sinful nature is egocentric. We all are born with unchangeable self-love. We love ourselves unconditionally—good or bad. The love that God intended Adam to express unconditionally toward others took a U-turn under sin and became self-centered.

Christ in Matthew 19 addresses a young man who has asked him, "What good thing must I do to be saved?" Jesus answers that just as we love ourselves unconditionally, we must show unconditional love toward our fellow man.

This is impossible through human effort and comes only through the power of the gospel. Paul says that when Christians stand under the umbrella of justification by faith, they not only have peace with God but experience transformation of life. Christian life in terms of human relationships is a life of love. When Christians love one another, they fulfill the law by reflecting, producing, and experiencing the fruits of the Spirit—love, joy, peace, long-suffering, temperance and so forth, against which the law says nothing (Galatians 5:22-24).

Christian Teeth Marks

Paul ends Galatians 5:15 with the words, "But if you bite and devour one another. . . ." Legalism always produces backbiting. The moment we seek salvation under the umbrella of legalism, we stop looking at Christ and begin examining and comparing ourselves to others.

But under grace, all of us acknowledge that we are 100 percent sinners, saved by grace. There is then absolutely no point in comparing ourselves with one another, for we are all in the same position, totally depraved, saved by grace. Our hearts are all filled with joy and gratitude.

But legalism concentrates only on performance, and Christians' performances vary widely. A legalist seizes on this discrepancy and compares himself with those who are less successful. This attitude ignites controversy, strife, judging, and backbiting.

Paul tells the Galatians that any church that returns to legalism will lose its loving ways and become filled with jealousy, backbiting, gossip, and judging.

Three "L" Words

The Christian life is neither a life of *legalism* nor a life of *license*. It is a life of *liberty*. And with Christian liberty come love-motivated responsibilities. These responsibilities are twofold.

First, Christians will determine to do nothing to diminish their relationship to God (Romans 14:7-8); and *second*, Christian responsibility means doing nothing that will cause a fellow believer to stumble (1 Corinthians 10:31-33).

On the one hand, Christians live lives pleasing to God. On the other, they do nothing that causes fellow believers to move away from Christ.

True Christian liberty means freedom to live lives of loving service and self-control. Satan's two traps—license and legalism, are both gospel counterfeits. They may resemble the gospel, but both are perversions.

May all believers who read this book remain on that narrow road that leads to heaven—that narrow road which is Christ and Him crucified.

Christianity has often earned a bad name because too many

Christians have failed to live the Christian life—love for God and love for their fellowmen. May it never be said among us that Christianity has opened the door to license.

Chapter 13
Spirit vs Flesh
Galatians 5:16-26

Luke's gospel tells of a Sabbath-day's visit Christ makes to his hometown synagogue in Nazareth. A priest hands him a scroll to read, and Jesus turns to the verses we find today in Isaiah 61:1 and 2.

To introduce this study, let us read those words of Jesus: "'The Spirit of the Lord is upon Me, because he has anointed Me to preach the gospel to the poor. He has sent me to heal the brokenhearted, To preach deliverance to the captives, And recovery of sight to the blind, To set at liberty those who are oppressed, To preach the acceptable year of the Lord.' Then he closed the book, and gave it back to the attendant and sat down. And the eyes of all who were in the synagogue were fixed on Him. And He began to say to them, 'Today, this scripture is fulfilled in your hearing.'"

Christ came to set humanity free—but free from what? The apostle Paul proclaims in Romans and Galatians 5:1-15 that Christ frees sinners from the condemnation of the law and the slavery of sin.

This freedom, as we see in Galatians 5:13-15, does not give license to sin but sets the believer free to live a life of self-control and loving service. But how can such a life be lived? Many sincere Christians ask this question: "We appreciate the assurance of salvation we find in the gospel," they say, "but how do we live the Christian life of self-control and loving service? We are still struggling in our Christian experience!"

Living the Christian Life

Galatians 5:16-26 answers that question. But before we

examine this passage, let us look at what takes place in Christians at conversion, when they accept Jesus Christ as Savior.

Conversion basically consists of a change of mind. The English Bible calls it repentance, but the original Greek term literally means a change of mind. But nothing changes in the believer's physical body at conversion—his natural bent to selfishness (sin) remains as strong as ever.

In Ephesians 2:3 Paul says that before conversion, a nonbeliever's mind and body are in one accord, both dedicated to one's personal advancement and pleasure. But in the new believer, according to Romans 7:15-25, mind and body are at war.

Besides a change of mind, however, "regeneration" or a "new birth" also occurs at conversion. According to 2 Peter 1:2-4, new believers become partakers of the divine nature. In Jesus' dialogue with Nicodemus in John 3:5-8, he tells the Jewish aristocrat, "Nicodemus, you need to be born again. You need to be born from above. You need to be born of the Spirit."

Internal Tension

Every genuine believer goes through these two experiences—a change of mind and a new-birth experience. This creates internal tension, and Paul graphically describes this struggle in Romans 7:15-24.

How, then, can Christians overcome the flesh? Or must they live in frustrated tension between their converted minds and sinful desires?

Faced with such turmoil, many new Christians question their own conversion. What they may not realize is that tension between flesh and Spirit is a good sign—strong evidence of conversion. The *absence* of tension is a much more worrisome sign.

Is it possible, then, to subdue the flesh through consecrated willpower? Romans 7 proves beyond a shadow of doubt that converted minds, no matter how sincere or strong willed, cannot of themselves conquer the flesh. Willpower may subdue the flesh for a season, but it can never overcome it, according to Paul in Romans 7:24: “O wretched man that I am! Who will deliver me from this body of death (*this body dominated by sin)*?” Paul knows he can never subdue his flesh alone, and he cries heavenward: “I thank God, through Jesus Christ (*the flesh can be conquered*).”

How does Jesus do it? Galatians 5:16-26 provides the answer. Here Paul makes it absolutely clear that the indwelling Spirit can indeed mortify the deeds of the flesh: “I say, then: Walk in the Spirit, and you shall not fulfill the lusts of the flesh. For the flesh lusts against the Spirit, and the Spirit against the flesh; and these are contrary to one another, so that you do not do the things that you wish. But if you are led by the Spirit, you are not under the law. Now the works of the flesh are evident, which are adultery, fornication, uncleanness, licentiousness, idolatry, sorcery, hatred, contentions, jealousies, outbursts of wrath, selfish ambitions, dissensions, heresies, envy, murders, drunkenness, revelries, and the like; of which I tell you beforehand, just as I also told you in time past, that those who practice such things will not inherit the kingdom of God. But, the fruit of the Spirit is love, joy, peace, long-suffering, kindness, goodness, faithfulness, gentleness, self-control. Against such there is no law. And those who are Christ’s have crucified the flesh with its passion and desires. If we live in the Spirit, let us also walk in the Spirit. Let us not become conceited, provoking one another, envying one another.”

Fruits of the Gospel

Christian living is the result, or fruits, of the gospel; it makes no contribution to one’s acceptance before God. The doing and dying of Jesus Christ accomplished this—nothing else. But the Galatians had become sidetracked from this wonderful truth and submitted to the false teachings of Judaizers who said that besides believing in Christ, one must be circumcised and keep the law of Moses. Christian living, wonderful as it may be, contributes not one iota toward salvation. It carries no merit. Christian living is the fruits of the gospel, evidence of salvation that has already occurred. The Christian is perfect in Christ through faith in His life and death, through His shed blood.

"I say then, walk in the Spirit and you shall not fulfill the lust of the flesh," Paul says. In verse 17, then, he describes the tremendous struggle between the flesh and the spirit: "The flesh lusts against the Spirit and the Spirit against the flesh and these are contrary one to another so that you do not do the things you wish."

Verse 17, if read alone, appears to say that Christians are incapable of living godly lives. But when read as an explanation of verse 16, the two verses together affirm that Christians who walk in the Spirit will not fulfill the lusts of the flesh. Paul is not talking about walking by willpower, for the will cannot conquer the flesh. Only when Christians walk in the Spirit can the lusts of the flesh be controlled.

Is it possible, then, to say "No" to the flesh? The mind may be able to say "No" to the flesh for a season, but sooner or later the flesh takes over, leading them to do what their converted minds hate to do. This is the Romans 7 experience.

What Paul is saying in Galatians 5:16 and Romans 8:5 onward is that if Christians walk in the Spirit and allow the Holy Spirit to control their minds, the flesh will indeed be subdued and conquered.

Galatians 5:19 adds helpful insight: "Now the works of the flesh are evident which are adultery, fornication, uncleanness, licentiousness . . . (*Paul lists a string of sinful acts*)."

Notice that these sinful acts are referred to as "works of the flesh." Paul says in Romans 8:9 onward that Christians are not of the flesh, for they have accepted Jesus Christ as their Savior. They are born-again Christians, walking in the Spirit. And if Christians walk in the Spirit and are led by the Spirit, Paul says in verse 18 "you are not under the law." To be under the law means to live under the jurisdiction of the law. To live under the jurisdiction of the law means they must obey the law in and of themselves to be saved. To be under law means that they must, by their own effort, obey it perfectly. If they disobey, they will die.

The Holy Spirit is given only to those who have accepted Jesus Christ as their Savior, under the umbrella of justification by faith alone. Paul asks these questions in Galatians 3:1 and 2: "This only I want to learn from you. Did you receive the Spirit by the works of the law or by the hearing of faith? Are you so foolish that having begun in the Spirit, are you now being made perfect by the flesh?"

God gives His Spirit only to those who recognize that they are total sinners—100 percent sinners, incapable of saving themselves. The Holy Spirit does not produce righteousness in order to save the Christian—He is not a Co-redeemer with Christ. The Christian is saved by the doing and dying of Christ—nothing else. The work of the Holy Spirit is to make this salvation come alive in the Christian's life. Salvation in Jesus includes salvation from the guilt and punishment of sin, salvation from the power of and slavery to sin, and salvation from the presence and nature of sin. The Holy Spirit working in the Christian produces this reality within them.

The moment Christians accept Jesus Christ by faith, the Holy Spirit comes and dwells in them. They experience the new birth, or regeneration. The Holy Spirit convinces the new believers that they are children of God; set free from the slavery of sin by the Lord, Jesus Christ.

The Holy Spirit also works to subdue and conquer the flesh so that the will of God becomes a reality as the Christian walks in the Spirit. Finally, at the Second Coming of Christ, the sinful body of corruption will put on incorruption (1 Corinthians 15:50-54).

Sanctification

What Paul is dealing with in Galatians 5 is known as sanctification—Christian living. From beginning to end, the walk of the Christian is a walk of faith. They are justified by faith alone. They are sanctified by faith alone. But in Christian living, faith is always a struggle. Faith is saying, "Not I, but Christ." By nature human beings are self-dependent and egocentric; so, to submit to Christ's will is a struggle. Paul calls it a fight of faith.

Faith is not simply a mental assent to truth. Faith is saying, "I am crucified with Christ." In other words, "I have been executed" or, as Paul says in Romans 6:6, the old, egocentric, Adam-like self life dies with Christ on the cross. In exchange the Christian accepts the life of Christ which He gave at the cross.

Two things took place at the cross and the resurrection: First, the corporate life of the human race died, eternally in Christ under God's law (Galatians 2:19). Paul says in Romans 6:7, "He that is dead to sin is freed (*in Greek 'justified'*) from sin." He says in Romans 7:1 that the law has dominion over a person only so long as he or she is alive. The moment the person by faith and baptism identifies with the death of Christ, he or she is freed from the jurisdiction of the law. The law was not done away with at the cross. *Humanity* was done away with (Romans 7:4). The old life was done away with. In exchange, the believer receives a new life (the life of Christ given to humanity in the resurrection, 1 John 5:11).

Fundamental Principles

We find these sublime statements in Galatians 2:20: "I am crucified with Christ, nevertheless, I live, but the life I now live, I live by faith in the Son of God who loved me and gave himself for me," and "It is not I but Christ who lives in me."

These are the fundamental principles of genuine Christianity. From beginning to end the gospel formula is the same, "Not I, but Christ."

When Paul says, "I am crucified with Christ," in Galatians 2:20, he uses the perfect tense, which in Greek means something that took place in the past but is still going on.

When believers accept Christ, they submit to something that took place at the cross. But the effect of that submission goes on throughout their lives. It is like marriage vows. When a man and woman marry, they declare vows to each other—once. But they live by those vows throughout their married life. The Christian, likewise, must practice what he has submitted to by faith when he came to Christ. He must walk in the Spirit.

Walking in the Spirit

Paul explains "walking in the Spirit" in Romans 8:5 and onward. The minds of those walking in the Spirit are preoccupied with the things of the Spirit, while the minds of those walking in the flesh are preoccupied with the things of the flesh. This is not hard to explain. A converted, born-again Christian has two natures. He has the old nature, which is dead by faith but in reality is still there; and he has a new, born-again nature. Both natures have built-in desires. The flesh wants to sin. The Spirit wants to live a life pleasing to God. Neither nature can do what it wants without the consent of the mind.

When a Christian is walking in the Spirit, preoccupied with spiritual things, praying without ceasing (which means keeping the mind totally connected with the Spirit), the Spirit gives the mind power to say "No" to the flesh. Since the Spirit of Christ is stronger than the law of sin and death, the Spirit will gain victory every time (Romans 8:3 and 11).

But the Spirit does more than gain victory; it also produces fruit. Galatians 5:22 makes it clear that Christian living does not consist of works but fruit bearing. The flesh produces works on its own, but that which the Holy Spirit produces does not originate within the believers, or through them. Yes, the fruit is produced *in* the believers, but the Source of that holy, righteous living is the Holy Spirit. This fruit consists of love, joy, peace, long-suffering, and so on, "against such there is no law" (Galatians 5:23). Therefore what we fail to do under law we can now do under grace.

Crucified Flesh

Paul ends Galatians 5 by saying that those who belong to Christ have crucified the flesh with all its desires and passions. They must live by the Spirit, for Christianity is more than simply accepting Christ as Savior mentally, it is participating in Christ. To participate in Christ means saying constantly, "Not I, but Christ."

This is the truth that sets the Christian free—free not only from condemnation of the law but free to live a life pleasing to God.

In 2 Corinthians 3:17 and 18 Paul says that those who are set free in Christ, looking at themselves in Christ with open face, are transformed from glory to glory, even by the Spirit of the Lord.

Sin not only condemns us to death but has also robbed us of the glory of God (Romans 3:23). But the good news of the gospel not only saves the believer from the curse of the law (Galatians 3:13) but restores the glory of God in them (Colossians 1:27).

Chapter 14
Christian Relationships

Galatians 6:1-10

Paul's custom is always to end his epistles, or letters, with counsel or exhortation on Christian living, and Galatians is no exception.

The gospel, after all, is not some theory but the power of God unto salvation—salvation from sin, its guilt, its power, and its punishment. Its power transforms lives.

In Galatians 5:16-26, which we studied last chapter, the apostle Paul describes the Christians' struggle between flesh and Spirit and how victory comes by submitting the flesh to the cross of Christ and walking in the Spirit.

Now in Galatians 6:1-10, Paul describes how that victory over the flesh will affect relationships with others (Galatians 6:1-5) and the good done among others (Galatians 6:6-10).

We first look at Galatians 6:1-5: "Brethren, if a man is overtaken in any trespass, you who are spiritual restore such a one in a spirit of gentleness, considering yourself lest you also be tempted. Bear one another's burdens, and so fulfill the law of Christ. For if anyone thinks himself to be something, when he is nothing, he deceives himself. But let each one examine his own work, and then he will have rejoicing in himself alone and not in another."

Slipping and Falling

When Paul uses the word "brother" or "brethren," he means "fellow believers." He is now dealing with relationships among Christians in situations where a believer is caught in sin. The words "overtaken in any trespass" (KJV) are not words Paul commonly applies to sin as a presence, or force. What he means here are slips or mishaps, as when someone slips and falls because of icy conditions. This contrasts sharply with a willful, deliberate decision to live a life of sin.

The apostle John brings out the same idea in 1 John 2:1. He says, "My little children, I am not telling you the good news of salvation so that you may condone sin." He uses the present continuous tense for the verb "sin." In other words, if anyone slips and falls—not because he wants to but because he has not yet learned to walk fully in the Spirit—how should we treat such a person? How should we treat a believer who has slipped? The answer is found in Galatians 6:1: "You who are spiritual, restore such a one in the spirit of gentleness, considering yourselves lest you also be tempted."

What does Paul mean by "You who are spiritual"? In the first three verses of 1 Corinthians 3 we discover that Paul divides all born-again Christians into two camps: The "carnal", or fleshly, and the "spiritual."

The passage reads, "And I, brethren, could not speak to you as to spiritual people but as to carnal, as to babes in Christ. I fed you with milk and not with solid food for until now you were not able to receive it and even now you are still not able, for you are still carnal. For where there are envy and strife and division among you, are you not carnal and behaving like mere men?"

Paul says that when we first come to Christ, we are babes in Him. Yes, we have become partakers of the divine nature. We are born-again Christians. We have experienced the new birth. But just as any human baby born with two legs must learn how to walk by falling many times, so a babe in Christ learning to walk in the Spirit is often carnal, controlled by the flesh.

The behavior of a carnal Christian, then (see 1 Corinthians 3:3), may to a large degree be similar to the behavior of an unconverted person. In Corinthians Paul rebukes Christians for remaining babes in Christ, though they were converted 10 years before.

Growing in Christ

How wonderful to have a baby in the home! Parents accept the need to change diapers for one, two, or even three years. But if after 10 years diapers are still being changed, something serious may be wrong with the child! This is the problem with the Corinthian church.

If a Christian, having experienced the new birth, is still walking in the flesh 10 years later, something is wrong. In Galatians 6 Paul is saying that mature Christians will always help immature Christians when they fall, just as parents help children who fall while learning to walk.

What, then, are the signs of maturity? A mature Christian is one who has lost all confidence in himself and says, "There is in me (*that is, in my flesh there is*) nothing good" (Romans 7:18). A mature Christian does not look down upon the person who has fallen but says to himself, "There go I but for the grace of God." This is the difference between a mature Christian and a legalist, for a legalist always compares himself with those who seem less successful.

Jesus and Sinners

We find an example of this in John 8:2-11. Jesus is preaching to a large, encircling crowd when suddenly a commotion begins at the edge of the circle. The crowd recognizes the commotion-makers, for they wear large boxes containing scriptural texts tied on their heads. They are Pharisees, and they are pushing the crowd aside, dragging a woman toward Jesus.

Jesus knows the commotion is being staged to try to discredit Him, but He watches quietly as the men drop the woman in front of Him and announce, in so many words, "Master (*not Messiah, but teacher*), Moses says that when anyone is caught in the act of adultery, they should be stoned. We have caught this woman in the very act. What is your verdict for her?"

Instead of replying, Jesus bends down and begins writing in the sand. The Pharisees think they had trapped Him at last, for if Jesus says, "Don't stone her," He will be breaking the Law of Moses. On the other hand, if He says, "Stone her," He will be going against the law of Rome. Either decision will get Him into trouble.

He looks up at them and makes an unexpected statement: "He that has no sin, let him throw the first stone."

Most English Bibles read this way. But the text in the original Greek language includes the definite article before the word "sin." So what Jesus is really saying is, "He that is without *the* sin, let him throw the first stone."

Jesus is not referring to just any kind of sin but specifically to adultery. How interesting that if indeed these Pharisees have caught her in the very act of adultery, where is the man? He is one of them!

Suddenly the Pharisees realize that Jesus can see through their facade. He can see through their masks and He knows that they are just as guilty as she is. One by one they walk away.

Spiritual Christians recognize that though they may not be committing acts of sin now, they are by nature 100 percent sinners, saved by grace.

There, But By the Grace of God. . .

The Jews of Jesus' day have failed to understand the spirit of the law of love. They keep the law only in the letter—the "dos" and "don'ts" and the rules they have made up. They see sin only as acts, forgetting that the law demands not only perfect acts but perfect motives.

Paul says in Romans 7:7 onward, "I did not know sin until the law showed me that thou shalt not covet."

Why does he choose that specific commandment? Because covetousness has nothing to do with an act but is a cherished desire that contradicts the will of God.

The Jews also fail to recognize a third definition that Paul brings out in Romans 7:20 and onward. Paul identifies within himself a force—a principle—he calls sin: "It is not I but sin that dwells in me." He calls it the law of sin (Romans 7:22-25).

All human beings are born with this bent to sin. Sinful acts are simply the outward evidence—the works—of what we are in the flesh, just as sanctification is the fruit of what Christians are in Jesus Christ.

Paul says here that Christians should bear one another's burdens because they belong to one body, just as when someone stubs a toe, the whole body bends to help. Christians should not view themselves as superior to others, for all are 100 percent sinners, saved by grace.

The Refrigerator of Christ

Paul illustrates this principle by comparing the church to a human body: "Ye are the body of Christ," he says. The body has many members but it is still one. Its members are vitally linked to the spiritual head of the church, Jesus Christ.

Now, let us imagine an everyday situation. Suppose my stomach is empty and craves nourishment. It sends a message to the head, "Head, I'm starving." So the head tells the legs, "Take this body to the fridge."

Interestingly enough, the legs do not say to the head: "I am not hungry! If the stomach is hungry, why doesn't it go to the fridge itself?"

The legs gladly take the body to the fridge, where the head orders the hands, "Open the door and bring the food out and feed the stomach."

The hands don't say to the head, "I am not hungry. I am tired. I want to rest. If the stomach wants to eat, it can feed itself!"

No, the hands submit to the head. And so it must be among Christians who are walking in the Spirit and applying the principle of the cross to their lives. They see the need of one as the need of all; the fault of one as the fault of all. Then, as with the stubbed toe, in gentleness, kindness, and love, they help restore spiritual wholeness to all. This is the power of the gospel (see Acts 4:32-35).

Sin's Divisiveness

Sin alienates mankind from God and human being from human being. It produces all kinds of divisions—racial, class, tribal, caste, color, political, ideological. All these divisions come from sin, the principle of self (Isaiah 53:6).

In New Testament times the world was divided between Jews and Gentiles, slaves and masters. New factions divide us today, but the gospel asks us to remove them all. In Paul's day it brought down every human barrier and replaced them with the brotherhood of mankind in Jesus Christ. There is no male and no female, no Jew or Gentile, no slave or master, no rich or poor, and no educated or uneducated. All are one in Christ in the Christian church (Galatians 3:28).

Gospel Proof

Jesus tells his disciples in John 13:34 and 35 that he wants them to love each other just as He has loved them—unconditionally, spontaneously. When the world sees self-emptying love reflected in the behavior of the believers, it will know they are His disciples.

We live in a scientific age that resists accepting anything—including the gospel—as a theory. Our world demands proof before accepting anything.

Many Eastern European countries adopted Marxism last century because Christianity had failed to reveal the life of Christ. Now Christianity is failing again in Rwanda, Bosnia and other countries.

Islam replaced Christianity as the primary Middle Eastern

religion some 1,400 years ago. Why? Because the Christian church had lost its saltiness and early power. Who was to blame? A Christian church that failed to demonstrate gospel power.

Paul is saying in Galatians 6 that if the gospel truly controls their lives, they are free—not just free from the condemnation of the law, but from the power and the slavery of self that dominates the unconverted (see 1 John 2:15 and 16). Only then can they love each other unconditionally as Jesus loves them.

Doing Good

Galatians 6:6-10 brings out a second result of walking in the Spirit. The Spirit-guided Christian not only carries a burden for other Christians—especially those who are struggling to learn to walk in the Spirit—but also goes about doing good.

Most Christians today find great difficulty reconciling grace with law, faith with works, because outwardly they seem mutually opposed.

This leads many who accept grace and faith to downplay law and works, and vice versa. While it is true that salvation comes by faith alone, the Bible definitely teaches that salvation comes by faith that works.

James 2:14 and 20 brings this out clearly: "Faith without works is dead." Genuine justification by faith always produces works.

Ephesians 2:8-10 puts this in a beautiful nutshell: "For by grace you have been saved through faith, and that not of yourselves; it is the gift of God, not of works, lest anyone should boast."

Christians are saved by grace alone through faith, and their works make no contribution whatever to their salvation. Verse 10 reads, "For we (*those who are justified by faith through grace*) are His workmanship, created in Christ Jesus for good works which God prepared beforehand that we should walk in them." The fruits of justification are good works.

Another passage from Paul's pen says the same thing, in Titus

2:14: "Who (*referring to Christ*) gave Himself for us that He might redeem us from every lawless deed and purify for Himself His own special people, zealous for good works."

Titus 3:5 adds: "Not by works of righteousness we have done but according to His mercy He saved us through the washing of regeneration and renewing of the Holy Spirit." This is how salvation really works!

In Titus 3:8, Paul adds, "This is a faithful saying and these things I want you to affirm constantly that those who have believed (*the born again Christian, justified by faith in Jesus Christ)* should be careful to maintain good works. These things are good and profitable to men (*the unsaved*)."

When Jesus was on earth, He went about doing good. Christians are to reflect the life of Christ, for their faith is more than a mental assent to truth. Christianity means participating in Jesus Christ. Christianity is saying, "Not I, but Christ," or "For me to live is Christ." The world no longer sees them but Christ living in them, the Hope of glory (Colossians 1:27).

Jesus says to his disciples in Matthew 5:14, "You are the light of the world." The "you" in the original appears in plural form. The word "light" is in the singular. We are many, but there is but one Light. That Light is Jesus Christ who shines in and through His followers (John 8:12).

Paul says in Galatians 6:6, "Let him who is taught the word share in all good things with him who teaches." God has chosen some as full-time preachers of the word, evangelizing the unchurched. These must survive in this world and Paul says, "Those who feed you spiritually, who bless you spiritually by the proclamation of the word, you in turn must share your material blessing with them."

Sowing and Reaping

In verse 7, then, Paul lays down a fundamental principle,

"Do not be deceived. God is not mocked. For whatsoever a man sows, that is what he will reap." This is a fundamental principle, in agriculture as in life. This immutable law operates in every sphere of life, in agriculture, in physics, and in daily living.

The story is told of a drunkard who became a great evangelist. One day someone asked him why he drank only carbonated water at church socials while others enjoyed banana splits and milkshakes. He replied, "When the Lord gave me a new heart at my conversion, He did not give me a new stomach."

God gives His followers new hearts. But they still have sinful natures and must struggle with the flesh until their dying day. The real question is, "How do they respond?"

Galatians 6:8 says: "For he who sows to his flesh, will of the flesh reap corruption. But he who sows to the Spirit will of the Spirit reap everlasting life."

Last study we looked at Romans 8, especially verses 5-14, where Paul says that the mind of the person walking in the flesh is preoccupied with fleshly things. But a Christian should not sow in the flesh. A farmer who plants corn expects corn in the harvest. He doesn't expect wheat. What we plant is what we can expect to reap.

Paul says in verses 9 and 10, "Let us not grow weary while doing good for in due season we shall reap if we do not lose heart. Therefore, as we have opportunity, let us do good to all, especially to those who are of the household of faith."

This is Christianity. It is the evidence of the power of the gospel in the lives of believers.

Chapter 15
Legalism vs. Gospel
Galatians 6:11-18

We now come to Paul's final words in Galatians. He has so far been dictating the epistle to a scribe—what we would call today a secretary. But now he takes the pen himself to add a personal postscript and to prove that this is truly his letter, not a forgery.

This is his custom, as he writes in 2 Thessalonians 3:17: "The salutation of Paul with my own hand, which is a sign in every epistle, so I write." Paul always signs his epistles with his own hand.

In Galatians 6:11-18, however, he writes several additional sentences with his own hand, for his heart is running over with love and anxiety: "See with what large letters I have written to you with my own hand! As many as desire to make a good showing in the flesh, these try to compel you to be circumcised, only that they may not suffer persecution for the cross of Christ. For not even those who are circumcised keep the law, but they desire to have you circumcised that they may glory in your flesh. But God forbid that I should glory except in the cross of our Lord Jesus Christ, by whom the world has been crucified to me, and I to the world. For in Christ Jesus neither circumcision nor uncircumcision avails anything, but a new creation. And as many as walk according to this rule, peace and mercy be upon them, and upon the Israel of God. From now on let no one trouble me, for I bear in my body the marks of the Lord Jesus. Brethren, the grace of our Lord Jesus Christ be with your spirit. Amen."

Large Letters

Notice how Paul begins in verse 11, "See with what large

letters I have written to you with my own hand." What is he trying to say?

Paul is saying in other words, "I am using large alphabet letters." He mentions this for three basic reasons: *First*, because of his poor eyesight, as already implied in Galatians 4:15; *second*, he is distressed about their sidetracking from the gospel and having accepted a subtle form of legalism; and *third*, he uses large letters because he wants to emphasize the importance of what he is saying. If Paul were writing this epistle today on a computer, he would bold-face, italicize, and even underline the words in these verses.

The issue in these lines is legalism versus the gospel, as it has been throughout the epistle. But here Paul shows how legalism and the gospel are opposites and cannot be mixed, synthesized, or reconciled. They are mutually exclusive. Paul makes it clear in Galatians 5:4 that the moment one adds law-keeping, circumcision, or good works as requirements for acceptance by God, one falls from grace. In other words, either Christ is the only basis of one's salvation or He is not a factor at all.

Major Differences

Before examining more closely Paul's final words in Galatians, let us look at three major differences between legalism and the gospel, as we prepare to study verses 12 to 18. Why are these two systems of salvation mutually exclusive?

First, legalism is primarily concerned with outward acts. Jesus reminds the Pharisees repeatedly: "Oh, yes, you wash the outside of the cup but inside you are dirty. You paint your tombs, whitewash them, so they look beautiful, but inside they are full of dead men's bones" (Matthew 23:5-28).

Legalism is concerned with outward performance. But God demands perfect acts *and* perfect motives. The gospel addresses the mind, or heart, and gospel transformation begins in the mind.

In the New Covenant the law of love becomes the basic drive of the Christian life as God writes it in the believers' hearts. In the Old Covenant, the law is simply written on tables of stone—a list of rules.

Second, legalism satisfies egocentric concerns and basic human nature. Because of sin, human beings are by nature controlled by pride. Legalism provides natural satisfaction for human pride. But the gospel crucifies the flesh with all its pride (Galatians 5:24).

Third and finally, legalism is salvation by "my own good works." The gospel is salvation by grace alone. True, salvation by grace alone does indeed produce good works in the believers. But these works make no contribution to their acceptance before God or their justification. Paul clearly says in Galatians 2:16: "By the works of the law shall no flesh be justified." Believers are justified by faith alone in the perfect life and death of Jesus Christ. We must keep these major differences in mind as we study the next few verses.

Paul's Final Words

"As many as desire to make a good showing in the flesh," Paul says in Galatians 6:12. In other words, "Those who want to brag about what they have accomplished insist that you should be circumcised only that they may not suffer persecution for the cross of Christ."

Paul is saying here that the flesh likes to brag about what it accomplishes. "Glory for me" lies at the very heart foundation of sinful nature. The cross, on the other hand, casts the glory of man in the dust and gives no credit whatever to human nature.

The cross is God's verdict about man's sinful nature. Human pride does not like its own glory trampled in the dust. So the cross becomes an offense, a hindrance to human pride. The legalist hates the cross of Christ, for it is God's verdict against the flesh. The flesh has no salvage value after the cross (Galatians 5:24).

Paul says in verse 13, "For not even those who are circumcised keep the law, but they desire to have you circumcised that they may glory in your flesh."

Those who insist that believers must keep the law and be circumcised cannot even meet their own standards—yet they want to foist these requirements on others! Jesus told His disciples that the Pharisees heaped burdens on others they themselves could not carry. Why? So they can brag about what they had required others to do: "See how many souls we have won."

Soul winning is not the work of man; it is the work of the Holy Spirit. Christians can only witness for Jesus Christ. Human beings should never take credit for soul winning to themselves—but the flesh chafes at giving the glory to God.

Paul's Boasting

Paul now writes in verse 14, "But God forbid (*it is unthinkable*) that I should glory (*or boast*) except in the cross of our Lord Jesus Christ, by whom the world has been crucified to me and I to the world."

What a powerful statement! Paul finds it unthinkable that a genuine Christian should find glory in anything but Jesus Christ and Him crucified. The word "boast" or "glory" is not as strong here as it is in the original Greek. Paul says here that the cross of Christ is *everything.*

What does the cross mean to Paul? It means that he is crucified to the world and the world is crucified to him. When a person is executed on a cross the world says he is eternally finished. But Paul says, "When I accept the cross of Christ, it is not only the world that says good-bye to me but I say good-bye to the world."

Paul's "World"

What does Paul mean by the "world"? Does he mean he must now live in a monastery away from the world? No, Paul is not making the monastic mistake of later generations. Paul's definition for "world" is the same as the one found in 1 John 2:15-17 and passages such as James 1:27 and James 4. Jesus made it clear to the disciples that they would have a function *in* the world. Paul uses the word "world" in the same sense as 1 John 2:15-17: "Do not love the world or the things in the world. If anyone loves the world, the love of the Father is not in him. For all that is in the world the lust of the flesh (*sinful desires of human nature*), the lust of the eyes (*the sin of covetousness*) and the pride of life (*the desire to be first*) is not of the Father but is of the world. And the world is passing away and the lust of it; but he who does the will of God, abides forever."

The word "world" here refers to three basic drives that control every unbeliever—the lust of the flesh, the lust of the eyes, and the pride of life.

Paul says in Galatians 5:24 that those who belong to Christ have crucified the flesh and its desires. Genuine Christians who have submitted to the cross of Christ no longer allow these three basic drives to be dominating factors in their lives. A Christian is no longer to be controlled by the lust of the flesh, the lust of the eyes, and the pride of life. The Christian demonstrates the love of God by going about doing good to others.

Paul is saying that a Christian is one who glories in the cross because the cross has liberated him from these principles of sin—love of self, lust of the eyes, and the pride of life.

Now Paul continues, "By whom the world has been crucified unto me and I to the world." Paul is saying that when Christians accept Christ, obey the gospel, and surrender to the cross of Christ, a dramatic change of allegiance takes place.

When I became an American citizen, I had to relinquish my British citizenship. I had to give up all allegiance to foreign potentates and pledge loyalty to the American government. So it is with Christians who change their citizenship from this world (under Satan) to heaven (under Christ).

A Christian is more than a person who has been forgiven, justified, and achieved peace with God. A Christian actually changes citizenship. Jesus says to the disciples in John 15:18,19: "You are not of the world but I have chosen you out of the world."

The apostle John in 1 John 5:19 divides the human race into two camps. "We belong to God," he says of Christians. But of unbelievers he says, "the whole world lies under the wicked one." Christians are citizens of heaven who are still living in Satan's territory. On a spiritual plane they are foreigners in this world, citizens of heaven.

How tragic that much of the world today is creeping into the church. Christians are borrowing the world's ideas and depending on its resources. When the world moves in a certain direction, the church follows a few years later. Look at divorce and abortion—these worldly ideas have become accepted and commonplace in many churches. This should never be. The cross of Christ excludes everything that is of the world from the church.

Paul predicts this falling-away in 2 Timothy 3:15, writing that the time will come before the end when the church will have a form of godliness but deny the power thereof. I challenge all Christians to renew their commitment to total spiritual separation from the world.

Jesus' Perfect Work

Paul now summarizes his epistle in Galatians 6:15, "For in Christ Jesus, neither circumcision nor uncircumcision avails anything."

Whatever Christians do or don't do makes no contribution toward their salvation in Christ Jesus. Why? Because the salvation that Jesus obtained in His doing and in His dying was perfect and complete. When Jesus cried on the cross, "It is finished," He meant that salvation, full and complete, was finished. No one can improve on it, no one can add to it. It must be accepted by faith with a heart full of gratitude for the wonderful redemption that God has obtained in His Son, Jesus Christ.

Christians must never try to add anything to the gospel. Many Christians who still misunderstand the gospel give the word "gospel" a very general meaning. When Jesus gave His disciples the great commission, "Go into all the world and preach this gospel to every creature," what did He mean by "gospel"?

Yes, we know the word means "good news." But what does that good news imply? The good news of the gospel is the birth, the life, the death, and the resurrection of the Lord, Jesus Christ. His followers can add nothing to these events. What God does in them—known as sanctification or holy living—is the *fruit* of the gospel. Finally, at His Second Coming, Christ will replace sinful nature in His followers with new, sinless natures. This we call glorification—the blessed hope and consummation of the gospel plan.

Once again, the gospel is the birth, life, death, and resurrection of Jesus Christ. Then come the *fruits* of the gospel—the evidence of a Christian's perfection in Christ. The Christian now stands justified in Christ, but he looks forward to glorification—the *hope* of the gospel, when this corruption puts on incorruption and this mortal puts on immortality.

Paul tells us that nothing Christians do avails anything toward their acceptance before God. They are accepted by God, declared righteous, and seen in Christ as if they had never sinned. In Christ they are new creatures.

Paul says in 2 Corinthians 5:17: "If any person is in Christ he is a new creation. The old is gone. The new is come."

The old belongs to sin. The new belongs to righteousness. The old comes under condemnation. The new comes under justification. The old tries to save itself but fails miserably. The new rests totally on what Jesus did 2,000 years ago.

A Final Plea

Having summarized the gospel, Paul in verses 16 to 18 concludes with a blessing and a plea: "And as many as walk according to this rule (*justification by faith alone, under the umbrella of grace alone*) may that person have peace and mercy from the God of Israel." Then he says, "From now on let no one trouble me, for I bear in my body the marks of the Lord Jesus."

It is not easy in Paul's day to be a Christian. To be a Christian is to risk persecution by Gentiles as well as Jews. Paul is challenging them here: "Please don't disappoint me. Don't give me more trouble. Remember that I gave up Judaism, accepted the gospel, and became an apostle at tremendous cost in suffering."

An instructive account of Paul's suffering appears in Acts 21: 27-30. Paul has just returned from his last missionary journey and has been advised by James to go through a seven-day purification process, for the Jews have accused him of opposing the Jewish law and people. The verses read, "So, after the seven days had been completed, the Jews from Asia seeing him (*Paul*) in the temple, stirred up the whole crowd and laid hands on him, crying out, Men of Israel, help! This is the man who teaches all men everywhere against the people, against the law, and this place; and furthermore he also brought Greeks (*Gentiles*) into the temple and has defiled this holy place. So they had previously seen Trophimus the Ephesian with him in the city, whom they supposed that Paul had brought into the temple. And all the city was disturbed; and the people ran together, seized Paul, and dragged him out of the temple; and immediately the doors were shut."

This is the story of Paul's life as a Christian. In 2 Corinthians 11:23 to 27 Paul summarizes what he has gone through for Christ. He tells of being shipwrecked, of being put in prison and of going through many things for Christ. But he still glories in Christ and is still willing to suffer for Christ.

Now in Galatians 6:18 he concludes, “Brethren, the grace of our Lord Jesus Christ be with your spirit. Amen.”

This is my prayer for all—that the grace of the Lord, Jesus Christ will be upon every Christian reading these words and that that none will ever be sidetracked from this wonderful truth of salvation by grace alone.

Chapter 16
The Two Counterfeits
Conclusion

No one hates the gospel of the Lord, Jesus Christ more than Satan does, for the gospel is the only strategy that has been able to defeat him on earth and deprive him of his citizens.

Paul points out in 2 Corinthians 4:3 and 4 that Satan tries to prevent human beings from accepting the gospel: "But even if our gospel is veiled, it is veiled to those who are perishing, whose minds the god of this age (*Satan*) has blinded, who do not believe lest the light of the gospel of the glory of Christ who is the image of God, should shine on them."

Paul then expresses deep concern for the believers in 2 Corinthians 11:2-4: "For I am jealous for you with godly jealously. For I have betrothed you to one husband, that I may present you as a chaste virgin to Christ. But I fear lest somehow, as the serpent deceived Eve by his craftiness, so your minds may be corrupted from the simplicity that is in Christ. For if he who comes, preaches another Jesus whom we have not preached, or if you receive a different spirit which you have not received, or a different gospel which you have not accepted, you may well put up with it." Satan has indeed met with great success in sidetracking human beings from the pure gospel.

In this concluding chapter we look at the two major gospel counterfeits Satan presents to Christians—counterfeits he uses to counteract the power of the gospel, though both to some degree resemble the gospel.

These two counterfeits are known as legalism and antinomianism and we will look at each separately and in detail in this closing chapter.

Legalism

"Legalism" is an English term for which the Greek of the New Testament has no equivalent. Expressions used in the original New Testament Greek to denote "legalism" translate literally as "works of the law" or "deeds of the law." Paul uses these phrases when he writes about those who seek to attain salvation by doing good works or by keeping the law.

"Legalism", then, means to use the law of God as a method or means of salvation. It is the fundamental principle of all non-Christian religions and is based on "dos" and "don'ts."

In its Christian form, legalism often resembles true salvation by grace, and the Galatians fell for the counterfeit even as the Jews had done 1,500 years before when they were given the gospel through the Old Testament Sanctuary service (Hebrews 4:2).

Both the Jews of old and the Galatians became sidetracked and trapped in legalism, as Paul himself was before his conversion to Christianity.

In Philippians 3:3 Paul says of every true Christian: "For we (*Christian believers*) are the circumcision who worship God in the Spirit, rejoice in Christ Jesus, and have no confidence in the flesh." A true Christian stands on the platform of "Not I, but Christ."

In Philippians 3: 4-6 Paul explains how, in his pre-converted condition, he could boast an impressive résumé of righteousness: he was circumcised eight days after birth, a Hebrew of notable pedigree, zealous for God, persecutor of the Christian church, blameless in keeping the letter of the law. In other words, he was the best.

Thank God, then, for verses 7-9! "But what things were gain to me, these I have counted loss for Christ. But indeed I also count all things loss for the excellency of the knowledge of Christ Jesus my Lord, for whom I have suffered the loss of all things, and count them as rubbish, that I may gain Christ and be found in Him, not having my own righteousness, which is from the law, but that which is through faith in Christ, the righteousness which is from God by faith."

Paul realizes that it all comes down to salvation either entirely by his own righteousness or by Christ's righteousness alone. When he realizes that his own righteousness is nothing but filthy rags, he is willing to give it all up for the righteousness of Christ, which comes through faith alone.

Legalism is man's way of trying to attain a ticket to heaven by his own performance, and Galatianism is a disguised form of legalism. In Galatianism a person begins by saying, "I accept Jesus Christ as my Savior." But grace alone is not enough for the Galatianist. Salvation for the Galatianist comes by grace *plus* keeping the Law of Moses.

Fruits of Law and Spirit

Any experience in the Christian's life, whether good works, acts of mercy, holy living, or obedience to the law, *in no way* contributes to his or her justification before God. All Christians must understand the difference between works of the law (legalism) and fruits of the Spirit (works of faith), if they are to avoid falling into the trap of legalism.

Martin Luther failed to understand this distinction at the beginning of his Reformation ministry—he could not see the difference between works of the law and works of faith, so he misinterprets James 2, especially verses 14 to the end of the chapter, where James says that genuine justification by faith always produces works. James never says, however, that these works *contribute* to justification—only that works are *evidence* of justification (see James 2:22).

In discussing good works, Paul deals primarily with works of the law—legalism. But he does address works of faith and says they are the work of God in the Christian (1 Thessalonians 1:2 and 3).

Take Romans 9:30-32. Here Paul makes it clear once again that works of the law contribute nothing to salvation. But in Romans 12 and 13 he goes on to say that genuine justification by faith transforms lives and produces people who go about doing good.

Two Major Differences

So what are the real differences between works of the law and works of faith? The Bible speaks of two major ones.

First, they come from *different sources*. Works of the law always originate from the flesh. The Bible refers to works of the law as self-righteousness. In Philippians 3:9 Paul describes the true Christian's attitude: "I want to be found in Christ not having my own righteousness."

"My own righteousness" means works of the law. The origin of works of the law is self—self-righteousness. In Isaiah 64:6 God declares that all human righteousness is as filthy rags, worthless.

In contrast, works of faith result from the Holy Spirit's presence within believers. These are not "*works*" but "*fruits.*" The fruits of the Spirit are love, joy, peace, long-suffering, and so on (Galatians 5:22-24). The major difference between works of the law and works of faith is their *origin*. One originates from self, the other from the indwelling of Christ—that is, the Holy Spirit.

Difference in Motivation

Second, the *motivation* for works of the law and works of faith lie at opposite poles. Selfishness always motivates works of the law. No matter how good these works appear outwardly, the underlying motive is to achieve salvation, praise, power, control, or commendation. Everything the flesh does—everything that originates from the sinful nature—is motivated by self-interest. (Ever heard the phrase, "I'm going to be good so I can go to heaven?")

Since the law of God demands not only perfect acts but perfect motives, legalism can never qualify a person for heaven. Paul says in Romans 3:20, "Therefore by the deeds of the law no flesh will be justified." The one and only thing the law does is show a sinner his or her sin. Once a person becomes a Christian, however, God writes the law of love in their minds, and the fruits of the Spirit become the fulfillment of that law.

Paul says in Galatians 5:23 that against such fruits there is no law, for the fruit of the Spirit is in harmony with the law. The motivation for works of the law is always self, whereas works of faith are motivated by the *agape* love of God.

In 1 Thessalonians 1:2 and 3 Paul commends the Thessalonians for their gift of love to the believers in Jerusalem. When the Holy Spirit produces His fruit, it is always motivated by love of God. Paul says in Galatians 5:14, "Love is the fulfillment of the law."

In Romans 13:10 he says, "All the law is fulfilled when we love our neighbors in the same way that we love ourselves."

We can see, then, that Paul is in full agreement with James, though they are writing primarily about two different things. We must not confuse works of the law with works of faith, as Luther did in his day. The law is given to unbelievers, not to save them, but to show them that they are sinners in need of grace. But when they become Christians—when they are justified by faith alone—the law becomes a standard of Christian living.

One certain way to recognize legalism when it lifts its ugly head is to accept the fact that all human beings, by nature, are totally sinful. Paul tells us in Romans 3:9-12, "There is none good, there is none righteous."

Speaking to Nicodemus, Jesus says, "That which is born of the flesh, is flesh." It is unchangeable. It is unredeemable. The flesh will not go to heaven. This corruption cannot inherit incorruption. For this reason we look forward to glorification—the redemption of the body (Romans 8:22 and 23; 1 Corinthians 15:50-54).

Antinomianism (Cheap Grace)

One of the gospel's greatest enemies is legalism—true—but a second counterfeit poses equal danger. The word "antinomianism" comes from two words put together: "Anti" means against. "Nomianism" comes from the Greek word "nomos", or the law. In trying to deliver the Galatians from legalism, Paul is fully aware that they could swing from legalism at one extreme to antinomianism on the other. Both are traps of Satan. They both resemble the gospel and are therefore counterfeits.

Unlike legalism, antinomianism says, "Since I am saved by grace alone, I can live as I please."

Let me expand on a personal experience I shared earlier in this book. While I was a missionary in Uganda, a young Ugandan came up to me. Now, I am of Indian ancestry and the Ugandan took me for a Hindu. Bless his heart, he wanted to share his faith!

So he asked me, "Are you saved?"

"Saved from what?" I challenged.

"Are you saved from sin?" he said.

"Can you be more specific?" I asked. "Are you talking of the guilt and punishment of sin, the power and slavery to sin, or the nature and presence of sin? Which one are you referring to?"

He looked at me and said, "You sound like a pastor!"

"I am!" I told him. "So, can I ask you the same question? Are you saved?"

He raised his arms and almost shouted with enthusiasm, "Praise the Lord, I was saved three months ago."

"How come?" I asked.

"Because I believed in Jesus Christ three months ago," he replied.

"Young man, can I correct you?" I asked. "You were not saved three months ago. You were saved 2,000 years ago. You accepted salvation three months ago. You were not saved *because* of your faith. Nowhere in the Bible does it say that. We are saved *through* or *by* faith. Faith is only an instrument, or channel, *by* which we receive Jesus Christ and His righteousness.

"In other words, it is Jesus Christ, the *object* of faith, that saves us. Faith does only one thing: It makes Christ's righteousness effective."

Then I added, "If you are justified by faith and if heaven is already yours, why do I smell a lot of beer on your breath?"

"Pastor," he said, "you know we are saved by grace and not by what we do."

"Really!" I replied. "Explain to me what you mean by salvation by grace alone."

"Very simple. Jesus did it all," he said.

He was absolutely right! Salvation comes from what Jesus did. But this Ugandan had taken the wonderful good news of salvation and perverted it into cheap grace, so I had to correct him.

I did this by asking him questions, just as Jesus did in His day: "You mean to say that I am saved because Jesus obeyed the law perfectly for me?" I asked.

"That's it!" he said.

"And He died in my place instead of me?"

"You have it now!" he replied.

"But I would like to take you one step further," I replied.

"What step?" he asked.

"Well, according to your argument, He also went to heaven instead of you."

The young man didn't like that, "No, no. I'm going to heaven," he assured me.

"If you are going to heaven, then you need to know the full message of grace," I replied. He had a little New Testament in his pocket and I asked him to turn to 2 Timothy 2:11.

I could have used many other texts, but I chose a passage that Paul gave to another young man, Timothy: "If we are to live with Christ, we must first die with Christ."

Too many Christians want to live with Christ without first dying with Christ. Accepting grace means dying to our old life (see Colossians 3:3).

We are all sinners, and die we must. We have no choice in this matter, or the gospel is not telling the truth. But if we accept our death in Christ, there is hope in the resurrection. If we choose to die outside of Christ, that is the end.

This is the difference between being born in this world and being born in the kingdom of God. Those born in this world are born sinners and are condemned to death because of Adam's rebellion. The ordinary person begins in this world with life and ends up with death.

But when believers enter the kingdom of God, the reverse occurs. They begin with death and end up with life. Unless Christians recognize this truth, they are perverting grace.

Paul makes a fascinating statement in Romans 5:20: "Where sin abounded, grace did much more abound." What does he mean?

He means it makes no difference how deeply a sinner falls into the pit of sin; grace is still able to save him. Grace is able to save Adolf Hitler, architect of the Holocaust. Grace is able to save Idi Amin, the greatest killer in Uganda's history.

But Paul realizes that people can take this statement and pervert it. The Christian can say, "Paul, you are saying that the more I sin, the more grace will cover my sins. Praise the Lord! Let us keep on sinning so we receive more and more grace!"

Paul deals with this problem in Romans 6 and asks, "Can we condone sin that grace may abound? Can we keep on sinning that grace may abound? Is this what I am teaching?" The answer is, "God forbid. How can we that died to sin, live any longer therein?"

The phrase "died to sin" occurs three times in Romans 6, applied twice to the believer and once to Christ. In verse 2 it applies to the believer who has been baptized into Christ.

In verse 10 Paul uses the same phrase in referring to Christ: "For the death that He died, He died to sin once for all." In other words, Jesus got rid of sin by His death. And now that he lives, he lives unto God.

In verse 11 Paul says to believers: "Likewise you also reckon yourselves to be dead indeed to sin and alive to God." Salvation by grace means identifying with the death, burial, and resurrection of Jesus Christ, as publicly confessed in baptism (Romans 6:3-8).

Becoming a Christian is not simply agreeing to a set of rules or joining a denomination. Christianity, at its very foundation, is participating in Jesus Christ, so Christians must be very careful not to take the gospel of grace and use it as an excuse to enjoy sin. Grace does not give any believer license to sin.

Ephesians 2:8-10 sums grace up in a nutshell: In verse 8 Paul says Christians are saved by grace and not of themselves, it is the gift of God received by faith.

In verse 9 he adds, "Not of works lest any one should boast." Believers are saved by grace alone, entirely as a gift from God. They make no contribution to their salvation.

Verse 10 continues, "For we are His (*God's*) workmanship, created in Christ Jesus for good works that we should now walk in it." In Colossians 2:10 Paul tells the believers that they are perfect in Christ. They are complete in Christ. But in verse 6, he says, "As you have therefore received Christ Jesus, the Lord, so walk in Him."

Genuine justification by faith gives no license to sin but transforms the life. It places new desires in the mind, creating the will to live a life pleasing to God.

Genuine justification is made clear in Galatians 2:20: "I have been crucified with Christ; it is no longer I who live, but Christ lives in me; and the life I now live in the flesh, I live by faith in the Son of God, who loved me and gave Himself for me." This is justification by faith. This is salvation by grace.

As I write this final paragraph, I pray that God will protect all believers from legalism in all its forms, on the one hand, and from cheap grace/antinomianism on the other. Both come from the camp of Satan. May we walk that narrow way called the gospel, avoiding the ditches of legalism and antinomianism, so we can say, “For me to live is Christ and if I have to die in the process, it is profit” (Philippians 1:21).

May this be your experience now and forevermore is my prayer in Jesus’ name, Amen.